D1264977

Visit to a Small Planet
and Other Television Plays

Visit to a Small Planet
and Other Television Plays

by
GORE VIDAL

Boston · Little, Brown and Company · *Toronto*

An adaptation of "Smoke" from *Dr. Martino and Other Stories* by
William Faulkner (Copyright 1934 by Random House, Inc.) and
an adaptation of "Barn Burning" from *Collected Stories of William
Faulkner* (Copyright 1939 by William Faulkner) are reprinted by
permission of Random House, Inc., and Columbia Broadcasting
System, Inc.

The script based on "The Turn of the Screw" by William James
is reprinted by permission of John Farquharson, Ltd., The Ford
Foundation (Copyright 1955 by The Ford Foundation) and
Paul R. Reynolds & Son.

The introduction is reprinted by permission of The New American
Library and has appeared in *New World Writing* (1956).

Visit to a Small Planet appeared in *Best Television Plays*, published
by Ballantine Books (1956).

*Published simultaneously in Canada
by Little, Brown & Company (Canada) Limited*

PRINTED IN THE UNITED STATES OF AMERICA

For Harold Franklin and Florence Britton

Contents

Foreword

Foreword

Until I began to write plays for television, I must confess that I entertained an amiable contempt for my stage-struck playwright friends who so meekly (masochistically, I often thought) submitted their talents to the irrelevant strictures of directors and stars, of newspapermen in Hartford and of sudden brief acquaintances in strange hotel rooms. I had taken to heart the failure of the prose writer in the theater: from Smollett's irritable attempts to get his tragedy produced to Henry James as he was jeered from the stage on his first night, the novelist has cut a ponderous, sad figure beneath the proscenium arch. As a novelist I was wary, preferring to suffer my reverses and petty triumphs on the familiar ground of prose and *not* in a theater, strewn already with the corpses of illustrious confreres.

The reason for our party's failure in what should have been a natural arena is caught in Flaubert's phrase: "The theatre is not an art but a secret." And the secret is deceptively simple: dialogue is not prose. It is another language and a talent for the novel does not necessarily mean a talent for the theater. The novel is the more private and (to me) the more satisfying art. A novel is all one's own, a world fashioned by a single intelligence, its reality in no way dependent upon the collective excellence of others. Also the mountebankery, the plain showmanship, which is necessary to playwriting inevitably strikes the novelist as disagreeably broad: you must show *every* collision on the stage, while in the novel it is often a virtue to avoid the obvious scene, to come at your great moments obliquely. Even dialogue is not the same in a novel as it is on the stage. Seldom can dialogue be taken from a book and played by actors. The reason is one of pace rather than of verisimilitude. Certainly, in our century, most novelists have an accurate ear for speech — it is a gift liberally bestowed on the good and the bad alike, the gray badge of naturalism — but in a novel *duration* differs from that of the stage. The novelist's arrangement of dialogue is seldom as concentrated as the playwright's, whose line must finally be achieved by real people talking, unassisted by an author's stage managing.

Aware of the essential difference between the novel and the play, I kept happily to my own country until the black winter of 1953, when I realized in a moment of revelation that the novel as a popular art form had come to a full halt. There were many reasons: television had stunned it; the new critics had laid it out all neat in a blue suit, a flower in its waxy hands ("Here lies the novel, explicated"), and the funeral orations were already under way in the literary quarterlies. The newspaper reviewers, lagging in their giddy way some twenty years behind the fact, wanted more Kipling and less art, while the public, its attention distracted by television and the movies, firmly refused to pay four dollars for anyone's novel, aware that

if a book had a good deal of healthy American sadism in
it they could eventually buy it in a cheap paper-backed
edition.

By 1953, unpopular novelists like myself were living
precariously on the bounty of reprint publishers, a bounty
which ended when those jolly opportunists managed to
flood the newsstands, sinking many, both good and bad.
Needless to say, none of this happened quickly; disaster
approached with stealthy tread and not until my revelation did I awaken to the harshness of the situation: that
I was on the verge of providing future thesis writers ("Ah,
yes, Gore Vidal . . . perhaps, Haskins, *you* can make
something out of him, though I liked your first project
better; I mean, Caroline poetry is something you can
get your teeth into") with a poignant page or two of met-
ropolitan suffering before I went off to Africa to run rifles,
never to be seen again.

But happily, when faced with ruin, all one's cunning and
resourcefulness rush to the surface and if one's career is
conducted beneath a beneficent star, crisis is healthy. I
looked about me. I had been a novelist for a decade. I had
been hailed as the peer of Voltaire, Henry James, Jack
London, Ronald Firbank and Frances Parkinson Keyes.
My early, least satisfactory works had adorned the best-
seller lists. Though not yet thirty years old, I was referred
to in the past tense as one of those novelists of the nine-
teen-forties from whom so much had been expected (it is
traditional that one's deliveries are not always noted at the
time). Alarmed, I turned to my peers to see what *they*
were doing. I discovered that the most colorful was writ-

ing unsuccessful musical comedies, while the most talented had virtuously contrived to die; the others had nearly all dropped from view, most of them finding dim employment either in anonymous journalism or in the Academy. The clever ones of course had married rich wives and traveled a lot. The prospect was not flooded with light.

But one must live, as they say, and since I do not write popular short stories or journalism or teach, and since I was monstrously spoiled by ten years of receiving money for the work I should have done whether I had been paid or not — the happiest of lives and the luckiest — it looked very much as if I should have to turn to the fantasy world of business and get a job. At that crucial moment, I discovered television.

I had not watched television until the winter I decided to write for it. At the time, its great advantage for me was proximity: I live on the banks of the Hudson River and there, to the south, in New York City, was this fine source of revenue. I was intrigued. I was soon enthralled. Right off, there is the immediacy of playwriting: there they are, your own creations, fleshed out by living people, the symbolic detail isolated by the camera as millions of strangers in their homes watch one's private vision made public. The day after my debut in February of 1954, I was hopelessly in love with writing plays for the camera. I discovered that although the restrictions imposed by a popular medium are not always agreeable they do at least make creative demands upon one's euphemistic talents and, more often than not, the tension between what one is not allowed to say and what one *must* say creates ingenious effects which, given total freedom, might never have been forced from the imagination. The only close analogy I can think of is the nineteenth-century novel: nearly all the productions of that bright age were published first in magazines edited for gentlewomen and supervised by Mrs. Grundy, her fist full of asterisks; there was so much the harried novelist could *not* say that he was impelled to freight heavily what he *could* say with other meanings, accomplishing the great things by indirection, through association and logical echo.

The same is true now in television. With a bit of patience and ingenuity there is nothing that the imaginative writer cannot say to the innocent millions. The naturalistic writer of course has a more difficult time. He is used to making his point directly and bluntly: you are a slut. There it is. And he becomes morose when he cannot bluntly hammer out the obvious the way he could on the stage or in the lower novel. But for my kind of second-story work, television is less confining. And of course the dramatic art is particularly satisfying for any writer with a polemical bent and I am at heart a propagandist, a tremendous hater, a tiresome nag, complacently positive that there is no human problem which could not be solved if people would simply do as I advise. This sort of intensity, no matter how idiotic, works well in the drama, if only because there is nothing more effective than having something — anything — to say.

As for the world of television, the notable characteristics are youth and enthusiasm. The dramatists, directors and producers are all young men and their deep pleasure in this new toy is communicable and heartening. There is none of the bored cynicism one often finds in Hollywood studios nor any of the rapacity and bad temper endemic to the theater in New York. Most television plays are bad, but considering that television uses up hundreds of new plays a year and that there have not been a hundred great plays written in the last two thousand years, they can be excused their failures if their intentions are honorable, and at the moment it is the very real sense of honor the better television writers possess which lends excitement and often dignity to their work.

Another novelty for me has been working with people. I had never before worked with anyone and the thought of belonging to a group was unnerving. But to my surprise I enjoyed it. Working on a play is not unlike being shipwrecked on an island with a group of strangers chosen at random from a foundered ship's company. For ten days actors, director, author, technicians work together, getting to know one another almost morbidly well. Then, when the play is over, sadly, sweetly, the players and the management separate, never to meet again . . . until the next play together.

An hour play on television of the sort I write is not filmed. It is performed at the exact moment it is seen on the air. The actors build their performances as they would on the stage; the only difference is that they are being photographed by three cameras and we, the audience, are watching a play as though it were a movie. What is called an hour play is about forty-seven minutes long, once the commercials are deducted. The camera directions which you will find in the scripts mean almost what they seem to say. *Dissolve* means going slowly out on one picture and in on another. A *fade-out* means the camera goes first to black and then begins again, from nothing, as it were, to fade in on a new scene. A *cut* is a quick shift from one picture to the next. A *beat* should be an unnecessary instruction since it is a note to the actor to pause in the midst of a speech, something he should do instinctively; however, in the early stages of rehearsal, it is often wise to make known the exact meaning of one's lines: it is not impossible to find an actor who has missed the entire point to his characterization and, abetted by a director, has blithely wrecked your play.

In the last three years I have written nearly thirty plays. I am by nature prodigal of what talents I possess, a fecundity not entirely admired in a century where a significant silence is often preferred to the work itself. One would dearly love more honor but, alas, I enjoy inventing. I have more ideas, more flashes of the thing done right in a day than I could ever record in a lifetime. However, all but seven of the television plays I have done have been either half-hour plays or adaptations. Incidentally, adapting is neither easier nor more difficult than writing an original play. There is, I think, only one basic trick to it and that, simply enough, is knowing how to read precisely, critically. One must get the idea, the fundamental *donnée,* of the work clearly established in one's own mind — the rest is simply a matter of taking the characters given and re-creating them in scenes of one's own fashioning.

I have collected these plays in the parental hope that

eventually some sort of repertory system will be evolved in television and certain plays will be done again from time to time, saving one's efforts from total oblivion. At the moment it is somewhat discouraging to see so many fine performances, so many good plays written, as it were, on air, nothing to show for all the work done but a kine-scope (a filmed record of the play) which, because of un-ions and technical considerations, is seldom shown again on television. It is a criminal waste of many talents and some day, perhaps on the new magnetic tape, a play which is broadcast live will be accurately recorded and reshown. After each of the plays in this volume, I have made some comment about the various problems encountered during production.

I have included five of the seven plays I have written for television. Of the twenty-odd adaptations, I have selected three. Some of the plays read better than others, but each played well, which is the most one can demand in a me-dium where viability is all. These plays were written at great speed and under great pressure. For some reason, I nearly always had two plays going at once: *A Sense of Justice* and *The Turn of the Screw* were in rehearsal at the same time; *Summer Pavilion* and *Visit to a Small Planet* were performed less than a week apart. There is no doubt that the work would have been better with more time, but time is the luxury in this medium.

Nevertheless, the voracity of television has, for all its limitations, created what is, I suspect, a golden age for the dramatist. There is so much air to be illustrated, so many eyes watching, so many fine technicians and interpreters at one's command that the playwright cannot help but thrive, and, who knows, from this great activity there may yet emerge a popular art whose beneficiary will be the age itself, casting a certain light over this dark century, revealing us not only as we are but as we might be.

Dark Possession

Performed February 15, 1954
on
Studio One (CBS)

Produced by Felix Jackson
Directed by Franklin Schaffner

The Cast

CHARLOTTE BELL WHEELER	Geraldine Fitzgerald
MRS. WICKS	Leora Thatcher
EMILY BELL	Barbara O'Neal
ANN BELL	Helen Auerbach
DR. ROGER WARING	Leslie Nielsen
GENERAL BELL	Bramwell Fletcher
MR. WESTON	Milton Selzer

Act One

Fade in on the drawing room of the house of General Richard Bell in Concord, New Hampshire. The year is 1911, but the room is in the solemn, cluttered style of the eighties. Through sliding mahogany doors at left is the hallway. At right is a fireplace with a mantel which supports figurines, an ormolu clock.

Superimpose title: THE YEAR IS 1911.

A close shot of Charlotte Wheeler's hands as she briskly opens letters at a tall secretary.

She pauses suddenly. Camera draws back, revealing her startled face. She is a handsome woman in her early forties. Mrs. Wicks, the elderly housekeeper, stands beside her.

MRS. WICKS (*reaching for letter*). Let me have it. I'll put it right in the fire. No use to upset ourselves with that filth.

CHARLOTTE (*grimly*). It can't be much worse than the others. (*Her eye scans the letter in her hand.*) It seems that this time I am a hypocrite, a wanton, a dishonest . . . (*She gasps and drops the letter.*)

MRS. WICKS. What is it? What on earth's the matter?

3

(Charlotte gets to her feet and rushes from the room, passing her older sister, Emily, at the door to the hall.)

EMILY. Good morning, Charlotte. I didn't get down to breakfast because . . . *(Emily turns and watches with surprise as Charlotte goes quickly up the stairs without a word.)* What's wrong, Mrs. Wicks?

MRS. WICKS *(picking up letter)*. It's another of those letters, Miss Emily.

EMILY. That makes seven altogether.

MRS. WICKS. Seven horrible letters out of nowhere!

EMILY. Out of some poison pen's mind. We must ignore them.

MRS. WICKS. But everyone in Concord loves Miss Charlotte. Who could possibly want to . . . to persecute her like this?

EMILY. I don't suppose there's any signature.

MRS. WICKS *(looks at letter, shakes head)*. The letter just breaks off, like the others did.

EMILY *(takes letter)*. Well, it doesn't seem much different from the rest. "Dishonest . . . hypocrite" . . . the Lord knows all this could apply to . . . *(Stops abruptly.)*

MRS. WICKS. What's the matter, Miss Emily?

EMILY. You didn't read it all, did you?

MRS. WICKS. No. I was going to throw it in the fire.

EMILY. Listen: "Only you and I know, Charlotte, what really happened to John. But soon others are going to find out. Soon even the police will know. The police will know *you* killed your husband."

(The two women look at one another in shocked silence.)

4

MRS. WICKS. What a terrible thing to say!

(*Emily folds the letter thoughtfully. She crosses to a nearby table where there is a photograph of John in a heavy silver frame.*)

EMILY. Do you remember when that was taken? It was the spring before he married Charlotte. (*Emily picks up the photograph and holds it, almost cradling it.*) We used to take long walks that spring, John and I, down by the lake. Mrs. Wicks, do you remember how he smiled?

MRS. WICKS. Very handsome, he was.

EMILY. I read him all of Sir Thomas More that spring while he sat on the grass and dreamed . . . oh, what a time it was! Until Charlotte came.

MRS. WICKS. Miss Charlotte and Mr. Wheeler were friends a long time before they were married.

EMILY. Not really, not the way we were those months.

MRS. WICKS (*sternly*). Emily, Charlotte and he were a happy couple. And now he's dead, and now these letters have started coming.

EMILY. Well, whoever's writing them knows altogether too much about us.

MRS. WICKS (*shocked*). How can you say such a thing?

EMILY. You know what I mean, Mrs. Wicks.

MRS. WICKS. Emily!

(*She glares at Emily. Ann enters the room, pushing their father's wheelchair. Ann is a dark, gentle girl in her twenties. General Bell is a disagreeable ancient.*)

ANN. Good morning, Emily. We missed you at breakfast.

EMILY. I had one of my headaches. Father, good morning.

(*The General does not answer.*)

ANN. Poor Emily, you've been having such a lot of them

5

lately. You must let Roger give you something. (*Looks about the dim room.*) Why does Charlotte keep this place like a tomb? We don't all have to stay in mourning. (*Throws the curtains open.*)

MRS. WICKS. I think the room's quite cheery. It's just the winter makes it dark.

GENERAL (*abruptly*). Ought to have a big breakfast.

EMILY. A cup of tea is all I need.

GENERAL. Tea! Need food on a day like this. (*Shivers.*) It's freezing in here.

MRS. WICKS. I'll put more wood on the fire.

(*She rolls him nearer the fireplace. She places a log on the fire.*)

ANN. It's color the room lacks. Oh! I know what would be wonderful! A stained-glass window, like the one the Wainwrights have in their parlor. It's so lovely in the morning, all lilac and yellow . . .

EMILY. When you're married you can have all the stained glass you like.

MRS. WICKS. Is Dr. Waring coming to take you downtown? (*Ann nods, goes to mirror, puts on hat.*)

ANN. He's coming by in his new carriage with the new horses . . . the ones he got all the way from Virginia . . . such a long way to go for horses. (*Looks at herself critically in mirror.*) Do I really look all right? I feel like I'm an old maid already.

MRS. WICKS (*glancing uneasily at Emily*). Nonsense. You're a child and that's that. As for being an old maid . . . well, there's no such thing until a woman's dead.

EMILY. That's very heartening, Mrs. Wicks.

ANN. Father *does* like Roger, doesn't he, Emily?

EMILY. Of course he likes him. You don't think he *enjoys* three grown daughters living with him, do you?

MRS. WICKS. The General would be lost without his girls, and you know it, Emily. *(Turns to Ann, maternally.)* He thinks Dr. Waring's a fine young man. He told me so himself.

GENERAL. Get a fire screen somebody. I'm half roasted. *(Emily adjusts fire screen for him.)*

MRS. WICKS. All that's in his favor, but even so . . .

EMILY *(returning).* I don't suppose Mrs. Wicks has told you, but there's been another letter.

ANN. Oh, no!

EMILY. Oh, yes! And whoever wrote it has accused Charlotte of killing John.

ANN. I don't believe it.

MRS. WICKS *(angrily).* There was no need of that. You didn't have to tell the child. And keep your voice down, Miss Emily. *(Looks anxiously at the General.)*

EMILY. She'll hear soon enough. Don't you understand what may happen?

MRS. WICKS. What may happen? Why, poor Miss Charlotte will lose her mind, that's what'll happen if we don't put a stop to these letters.

EMILY. That's not what I meant.

MRS. WICKS. All along I've wanted to take those filthy things to the police but no, Miss Charlotte says no use our doing that, no use washing family linen . . .

EMILY. We *can't* take them to the police even if we wanted to.

7

ANN. Why not?

EMILY. Because Charlotte has been accused of murder and we don't dare tell the police *that*.

ANN. I can't see why not. She didn't kill him, so why should we be afraid?

MRS. WICKS (*thoughtfully*). Miss Emily *does* have a point. I mean, the police might not understand . . . things.

ANN. I don't know what either of you is talking about. I've a mind to tell Father everything.

MRS. WICKS. Oh, you mustn't bother the General, child. He's too old for trouble now.

EMILY. He wouldn't do anything if he could.

ANN. I wish we'd told him when that first letter came, last spring.

EMILY. Well, we didn't and it's too late now.

ANN. Was Charlotte very much upset?

MRS. WICKS. Like lightning struck her, the poor lamb.

ANN. Then we'll have to go to the police. We'll have to find a way of stopping these letters.

EMILY. We don't dare.

(*The doorbell rings.*)

EMILY. That must be your young doctor. I'll let him in. (*Leaves the room.*)

GENERAL. Get me out of here!

ANN. Why, Father!

MRS. WICKS (*quickly*). It's much nicer in the sunroom. (*She starts to push him into the next room, but he pulls away from her, operating the wheelchair himself.*)

GENERAL. I'll manage . . . house full of strangers.

8

(He goes. Mrs. Wicks turns to Ann.)

MRS. WICKS. Don't you go brood about the General's bad temper. Keep your mind on your business.

(Roger Waring, blond and hearty, enters.)

ROGER. Good morning, Mrs. Wicks . . . Ann.

ANN. Oh, Roger, I . . . I'm almost ready.

MRS. WICKS. We're expecting you tonight for dinner, aren't we, Doctor?

ROGER. I believe so.

MRS. WICKS. Well, I better look in on the kitchen. The General's coming down for dinner, too. Feeling much better these days, though he complains of the cold.

(Mrs. Wicks leaves the room. Roger and Ann smile awkwardly at one another. They are standing in the doorway of the hall.)

ROGER. They're outside . . . the new horses.

ANN *(distractedly).* Oh, good! I'm glad.

ROGER. What's wrong? You did say you wanted me to pick you up.

ANN. Of course, and I'm almost ready. It's just that . . . *(In a rush.)* Roger, I *have* to tell you. You've got to help us.

ROGER *(bewildered).* Why, certainly, but . . .

ANN. Someone has been writing Charlotte the most awful letters. *(She opens secretary drawer.)* We don't know who it is. This one came today. *(She hands him the letter.)*

ROGER. Odd, looks as though it had been held up to a mirror and copied.

ANN *(as he reads).* Each letter's worse than the one before.

9

They say terrible things about all of us, but mostly they attack poor Charlotte. It's got so she can't sleep at night. We're all worried about her . . . usually she's so serene . . . but now . . . well, she's showing the strain . . . sometimes when you speak to her she doesn't hear.

ROGER. That's quite a letter. Tell me about . . . the last part. How *did* her husband die?

ANN. He was an assistant district attorney. We all liked him, even Father did. Charlotte adored him. Four years ago he was found in his office, shot to death . . . with his own gun.

ROGER. They ever find who did it?

ANN. In a way . . . yes. Everyone knew, I mean, who did it. You see, he was prosecuting some extortionists. They said he'd never live to indict them.

ROGER. And they shot him?

ANN. Yes.

ROGER. But the actual murderer was never found?

ANN. No. The gang disappeared. No one saw any of them again.

ROGER. And Charlotte?

ANN. Nearly lost her mind. She never loved anyone but John in her life.

ROGER. And there was no suggestion that *she* might've . . . ?

ANN (*emphatically*). None! Until these letters started coming, until *this* letter.

ROGER (*excitedly*). Look! (*He shows her envelope.*)

ANN (*looks at it, bewildered*). I don't see anything. Just the address, and a stamp.

ROGER. But what else *should* there be?

ANN. Oh, why, there's no postmark!

ROGER. Which means the letter was never mailed.

ANN. But it came in the mail. I'm sure Mrs. Wicks brought the morning mail to Charlotte, the way she always does.

ROGER. Then don't you see what *that* means?

ANN. You think someone might have *brought* it here by hand?

ROGER. And run the risk of being caught? No. I think the letter was written by someone in this house.

ANN. But who? Why?

ROGER *(softly)*. Maybe it's better not to find out who or why.

ANN. You mean one of us is responsible? Someone here, in the family?

ROGER. Or in the house. *(Pause)*. Get a sample of the hand-writing of everyone in this house. Compare it to the letters.

ANN. All right. I'll try. *(Pauses; then, frightened.)* Someone . . . in this house . . .

> Roger puts one arm around Ann as we dis-
> solve to Charlotte pouring coffee in the din-
> ing room. Roger, Emily, Ann, General Bell
> are seated at the table. Mrs. Wicks is in and
> out.

CHARLOTTE. What do you like in your coffee, Dr. Waring?

ROGER. Just black . . . thank you.

EMILY. The doctors say that if you drink coffee at night . . .

ANN. Roger *is* a doctor, Emily.

CHARLOTTE *(smiling)*. Emily is a born physician. She pre-scribes for all of us.

ROGER. She's done pretty well. None of you looks in need of doctoring.

CHARLOTTE. You must find us very quiet after Boston.

ROGER. Not at all. (*Looks at Ann.*) Not now.

EMILY (*suddenly*). Dr. Waring is just being polite. We can't compare with Boston.

CHARLOTTE (*mildly*). Why, Emily! What a thing to say.

EMILY. John preferred Boston too. He never liked living here.

CHARLOTTE (*surprised*). John? You mean *my* John?

EMILY. The only one we've ever known, yes. When *I* was engaged to him, we talked of going away to Boston. He wanted to open a law office there.

(*A grim moment.*)

CHARLOTTE. Excuse me.

(*Charlotte rises and crosses to the General and gives him his coffee. Emily suddenly rises.*)

EMILY. I'll be right back.

(*She goes into the kitchen. Ann turns to Roger and whispers.*)

ANN. I checked everyone's handwriting. No one here could've written those letters.

ROGER. Handwriting can be disguised.

ANN. But there was nothing even close, nothing that . . .

CHARLOTTE (*returning*). Now don't be unsociable, Father. We don't want Dr. Waring to think us impolite, do we? (*The General grunts. Emily returns from the kitchen and takes her place at the table.*)

GENERAL (*suddenly*). Where's my pipe?

MRS. WICKS. You must've left it in the parlor.

GENERAL. I'll get it. You can't find anything. *(Starts to move to drawing-room doors. Mrs. Wicks pushes his chair as far as the door. He pulls away from her.)* Shut the door. *(Mrs. Wicks shuts the door.)*

CHARLOTTE *(to Roger).* We'd be lost without Mrs. Wicks. She's looked after all of us since we were children, since our mother died.

ROGER. You wouldn't like me to take you driving tomorrow? There's room for all of you.

CHARLOTTE. Not in Februrary. *(Smiles.)* The winter of our discontent.

EMILY. Summer and spring, too. *(She puts down her crocheting with an impatient gesture. To Roger.)* Wait until you've lived here year in and year out with nothing to do but eat and sleep and talk and write letters.
(On the word "letters" Ann and Roger look at one another involuntarily.)

CHARLOTTE. I've never heard you like this, Emily. *(To Roger.)* But February *can* be a bleak month in New Hampshire, Doctor. Spring seems an eternity away.

ROGER. I'm enjoying it.

EMILY. Then spring, then summer . . . *(Bitterly.)* I can tell you, Charlotte, if I'd married John we *would* have gone to Boston and he'd be alive today.

CHARLOTTE. I don't know what you're talking about.

EMILY. I think you do.

GENERAL *(from other room).* Mrs. Wicks! Mrs. Wicks!

MRS. WICKS. Yes, General.
(She hurries out of dining room, returning a moment later with the General. He has his pipe.)

13

ANN. Father, we saw Mayor Wainwright today. He sent you his regards.

GENERAL. Can't stand him.

MRS. WICKS. You know you like Mr. Wainwright.

GENERAL. No such thing. Not like the old days. We had different sort of men in public life. *(To Roger.)* You know the name Edward Everett?

ROGER. Yes, sir. He was from New Hampshire.

GENERAL. Friend of mine. Spoke at Gettysburg before Lincoln. Gave a better speech, I thought.

ROGER. Were you there, sir, at Gettysburg that day?

GENERAL. I commanded the Green Mountain Regiment. I heard all the speeches that day.

ROGER. That was a long time ago.

GENERAL *(dryly)*. A better time.

(While they speak, Charlotte has been staring at Emily.)

CHARLOTTE. You must have Dr. Waring prescribe something for you, dear. *(To Roger.)* Emily has been having headaches lately.

EMILY. No worse than usual.

ROGER. Perhaps you've been reading too much. Eye strain.

ANN. Or needlework. Emily is always doing something with her hands. She won second prize last year at the fair.

GENERAL *(suddenly)*. Messy thing, when two girls like the same fellow. Makes a lot of trouble.

(An uneasy moment.)

CHARLOTTE. Perhaps you should go to bed, Father. You know you're not to stay up late.

GENERAL. Perfectly happy sitting up, thank you.

MRS. WICKS *(bustling)*. It's almost ten o'clock, General. Miss Charlotte's right.

GENERAL. Haven't had a chance to talk to this young man yet. Don't want to go off like that . . . don't want to be rude. *(Chuckles maliciously.)*

CHARLOTTE *(standing)*. I think I'm a little tired, too. *(To Roger, who also stands.)* Don't go, Doctor, please. It's just that I've had such a . . . busy day.

ROGER. Of course.

CHARLOTTE *(smiling)*. I hope we'll see a great deal of you. Any time you want to come for dinner do . . . even on short notice.

ROGER. That's very kind of you.

CHARLOTTE. Good night.

(The others say good night. She leaves the room.)

ANN *(to Emily)*. That wasn't very nice . . . your talking about John to poor Charlotte.

EMILY. *Nice?* I don't think it was very nice when she . . .

> *There is a loud scream from Charlotte in the hall. Ann, Roger, Emily and Mrs. Wicks hurry into hall, where Charlotte is leaning on the console, her head bowed, sobbing. Ann, who gets to her first, gasps when she sees the mirror above the console. The camera moves in for a close shot of the mirror, on which is written, in giant letters scrawled in soap:* MURDERESS! *Fade out.*

Act Two

Fade in on Charlotte lying full length on the sofa in the drawing room. On her lap is an open book which she does not read. The expression on her face is sullen, unlike her usual self.

She gives a start when Mrs. Wicks enters the room with a glass of water and a vial of medicine which she puts on the table beside the couch.

MRS. WICKS. Time for your medicine. *(Looks at curtains.)* I wish you'd let me draw the curtains. It's the brightest day outside. *(She looks at Charlotte for response, but Charlotte ignores her.)* The General's keeping to his room today. *(She moves about, arranging, disarranging.)* You wouldn't like some tea, would you? No? Perhaps later, when Dr. Waring comes. He'll be glad to see you up, after last night. *(Charlotte smiles unpleasantly.)* I wanted to go to the police right then and there, but Miss Emily said no. She's wrong, too. We *must* have protection, that's what I said. We could all be killed in our beds, at this rate . . . strangers coming in the house, writing on mirrors. *(She looks at Charlotte's book.)* That doesn't seem a proper book for you, Miss

16

Charlotte. I've heard about those books in French. *(She indicates glass.)* Do take your medicine. *(Charlotte does not answer.)* It's going to be sad not having Miss Ann in the house, but then they'll live in Concord and he'll look after us. Such a fine doctor, too. We'd have been lost without him yesterday. *(She looks at the clock on the mantel.)* It's almost four. They'll be along any minute. *(Charlotte shudders suddenly. Mrs. Wicks notices this.)* It *is* chilly. I'll put more wood on the fire . . . it's been the coldest February.

(She puts log on fire. Charlotte in foreground follows her with her eyes. It is the first time she has shown any awareness of Mrs. Wicks's presence. Her expression is sly. When Mrs. Wicks returns, Charlotte looks quickly away.)

MRS. WICKS. Oh, it's going to be just like it was when you married Mr. Wheeler, when Ann marries the young doctor.

CHARLOTTE *(bitterly)*. When *I* married him?

MRS. WICKS. Married Mr. Wheeler, yes.

CHARLOTTE *(craftily)*. What do doctors carry in those black bags?

MRS. WICKS. Carry? Why, I don't know. Medicine, I suppose . . . things like that.

CHARLOTTE. *Strong* medicines?

MRS. WICKS. Strong? What do you mean?

CHARLOTTE. I wonder if they carry poison.

MRS. WICKS. What on earth's the matter with you? *(She sits down on the couch and takes Charlotte's hands in hers. She tries to look into her face, but Charlotte turns her*

17

head. *Mrs. Wicks is soothing.*) You mustn't even *think* of such things. Soon we'll find out who's been sending those letters and it will all be over, like a bad dream. Just be patient a little longer.

(The doorbell rings. Mrs. Wicks hurries from the room.)

MRS. WICKS. Don't forget your medicine.

(She slides the door open: a murmur of talk from the hallway. Charlotte sits up abruptly, takes the glass of water and hurls it into the curtains. Then, noiselessly, she buries her face in her hands. Roger and Ann enter together. He is carrying a black bag. He turns to Ann and nods. She leaves the room, shutting the door behind her. Roger crosses to the couch, pulls up a chair and sits down.)

ROGER *(gently).* Mrs. Wheeler? Mrs. Wheeler? *(Charlotte uncovers her face slowly and looks at him.)* I wanted to see you this morning but Ann said you were sleeping.

CHARLOTTE. I've only been up a short while.

ROGER *(takes her pulse).* It was a bad shock, I know.

CHARLOTTE. *Worse* than you know.

ROGER. You're much better today, I think. Why don't you let some sun in here?

CHARLOTTE. The light hurts my eyes.

ROGER. I wish you'd let me talk to your father about all this. . . .

CHARLOTTE. Oh, no! I couldn't have Father read those letters.

ROGER. But he must suspect something. He saw the mirror last night.

CHARLOTTE. I don't want him to read the letters.

18

ROGER. Then I think you should go to the police.

CHARLOTTE *(nods)*. If it could be done quietly. I don't think we . . . *I* can wait any longer.

ROGER. Would you like me to talk to them?

CHARLOTTE. No, I think I'd better.

ROGER. Soon?

CHARLOTTE. Soon.

ROGER. There's a possibility . . . well, the person might be dangerous.

CHARLOTTE. It's not really the letters I mind. It's the other things, the strange *little* things which keep happening, the . . . *(She stops, afraid to go on.)*

ROGER. The what?

CHARLOTTE. I'm being watched. Someone is watching me, and waiting. . . . I don't know why or for what, but I feel it, and there are times when I think I must be out of my mind.

ROGER. Well, you're not out of your mind, a stronger person than you . . .

CHARLOTTE *(not listening)*. Things of mine disappear, odds and ends of no value, except to me. And all the time the feeling that I am being watched by someone hiding, by someone waiting.

ROGER. You must have some idea who it is.

CHARLOTTE *(continuing)*. And now I think I will meet her soon, face to face, in some secret corner. And then I'll die. You see, whoever it is wants to kill me. I know it now.

(Roger sits back in his chair, startled, as Mrs. Wicks enters with tea tray.)

19

MRS. WICKS. Thought you'd both like some tea. *(Puts the tray down, pours two cups.)*

ROGER. That's good of you, Mrs. Wicks.

MRS. WICKS. Will you stay to dinner?

ROGER. I can't, thank you. But I'll come in afterwards, if I may.

MRS. WICKS. Of course. Now drink your tea, Miss Charlotte. *(To Roger.)* She wouldn't take her medicine. *(Leaves the room.)*

ROGER. Who *is* it? You must suspect someone.

CHARLOTTE *(slowly).* Yes, I do.

ROGER. Tell me.

CHARLOTTE. I can't. I don't dare. I *could* be wrong. There's no proof, none at all.

ROGER. Tell me about your husband.

CHARLOTTE *(calmly).* I loved him. They found him murdered one afternoon. You know the story, I'm sure.

ROGER. You don't mind talking about it?

CHARLOTTE. I mind very much. But I'll tell you anything you want to know.

ROGER. Was your sister Emily really in love with him?

CHARLOTTE. I don't know. I didn't think so at the time. I certainly didn't take him away from her. But thinking back I can see now that she might've been in love, in her strange way.

ROGER. Was she shy?

CHARLOTTE *(nodding).* With all men who were . . . eligible. But he was never interested in her. I know that. I think she's built all this up in her mind since. I'm sure she actually believes now that I stole him from her.

20

ROGER. What was it like, the day your husband was killed?

CHARLOTTE. Like no other day in my life! It was early autumn, the time of the equinox. That morning there was a storm. Ann was in Boston. Emily and I had lunch together here, with Father. We were all on edge.

ROGER. You lived in another place?

CHARLOTTE. We had a house, John and I, near the old Common.

ROGER. What time of day did he die?

CHARLOTTE. No one seems to know exactly. But sometime that afternoon. They found him in the early evening.

ROGER. And where were you and Emily *after* lunch?

CHARLOTTE *(thoughtfully)*. I don't remember. I really don't.

ROGER. Were you together?

CHARLOTTE. She says not, but I don't remember. I think I went a little mad when I was told he died.

ROGER. If there's anything you'd like me to do . . .

CHARLOTTE. You're very kind, but I have a feeling that won't be necessary. I think it will all be over soon. *Something* will happen.

ROGER. But what?

(Charlotte looks at him a long moment. Emily slides the door open.)

EMILY. Excuse me, Charlotte, but Father wants to see Dr. Waring for a moment. He's upstairs.

ROGER. I'll be right back.

CHARLOTTE. Don't bother about me. I'm all right. We'll see you after dinner. *(Picks up book with a surprised expression.)* A French novel! I wonder how I happened to get hold of this?

(Roger picks up his bag and leaves the room.)

CHARLOTTE. I'm going to the police, Emily, tomorrow morning.

EMILY. Do as you like.

CHARLOTTE. I can't stand any more of this.

EMILY. I'm sure you can't.

> *Emily goes into the dining room as we cut to the hallway. At the foot of the stairs, Roger and Ann talk.*

ROGER. Does your father really want to see me?

ANN. Yes. He's got a cold today. He also wants to discuss your intentions.

ROGER. Haven't you told him?

ANN *(laughs)*. Several times, but he never listens. . . . How is she?

ROGER. Disturbed, but in better shape than I would have thought, after last night.

ANN. She talked in her sleep all night long.

ROGER. Talked? But I gave her a strong sedative.

ANN. She . . . she's afraid someone will kill her, did you know that?

ROGER. Yes, she told me . . . and I think she knows who it is.

ANN *(whispering)*. So do I.

(Mrs. Wicks comes down the stairs, smiling.)

MRS. WICKS. The General's ready to see you now, Dr. Waring.

> *Dissolve to the drawing room. Emily crochets. Charlotte is seated on the sofa. The*

*room is cheerful with firelight. In the back-
ground, Ann pokes the fire absently. In the
foreground, the General, pushed by Mrs.
Wicks, is leaving the room.*

CHARLOTTE. Good night, Father.

GENERAL. Night.

MRS. WICKS *(to Charlotte)*. If you don't need me, I just
think I'll go to bed, after I look to the General.

CHARLOTTE. Of course.

(General and Mrs. Wicks go into the hall.)

CHARLOTTE *(to Ann)*. How did it go this afternoon — Father's talk with Roger?

ANN. Roger said they understand each other perfectly. It
seems Father talked politics and Roger listened. *(Doorbell rings.)* That must be Roger. *(She goes out of the
room, returns with Roger.)*

ROGER. Good evening, everyone.

CHARLOTTE. Good evening, Doctor. Ann, do get him some
brandy.

ROGER *(takes off coat)*. That sounds good. It's below zero.
By the way, are you expecting visitors?

CHARLOTTE. Visitors? Tonight? No, no one but you.

ROGER. That's odd. I thought I saw someone walking along
your driveway from the other side.

ANN. It's probably one of the servants.

CHARLOTTE. Was it a man . . . or a woman?

ROGER. A man, I think.

CHARLOTTE. Oh? Perhaps we should go see who it is. Perhaps . . .

(The sound of the doorbell ringing makes them all start. The three women look at one another in alarm. Roger goes into the hall, returns with Mr. Weston, a plain-clothesman.)

ROGER. This is Mr. Weston. He's with the police department.

WESTON *(apologetically)*. I was just passing by and thought I'd come in, Mrs. . . . Mrs. . . .

CHARLOTTE. I'm Mrs. Wheeler. These are my sisters.

WESTON. I recognize them, ma'am.

CHARLOTTE. What can we do for you, Mr. Weston?

EMILY. Take your coat off and sit down.

WESTON. Thank you. I'll only be a moment. I couldn't have a word with the General, could I?

CHARLOTTE. I'm afraid not. He's asleep.

WESTON. Well, I guess it can keep.

CHARLOTTE. I'm afraid it won't.

WESTON. You . . . know?

CHARLOTTE. I think so.

EMILY. Charlotte!

CHARLOTTE. You've received an anonymous letter, haven't you?

WESTON. Why . . . yes, ma'am, that's right. How did you . . .

CHARLOTTE. I've been sent several, which you're welcome to read.

WESTON. It's not that we pay any mind to what they *say* — they're crazy all right — but we figured we ought to investigate, find out who's responsible.

CHARLOTTE. I hope you can. I'd intended to see you about them.

WESTON. The letter said you probably would.
(Charlotte looks at him, astonished.)
CHARLOTTE. Said *what?*
WESTON. Said you'd probably come tell us your side of the case . . . oh, it was some letter all right!
CHARLOTTE. But who could have known I was ready to go to the police? I didn't tell anyone except . . . *(Stops abruptly.)*
ROGER. I suggest, officer, you see Mrs. Wheeler another time. As her doctor . . .
CHARLOTTE. That's all right. *(To Weston.)* I can imagine what the letter said. I'm supposed to have murdered my husband, isn't that right?
WESTON *(uncomfortably)*. Well, yes, ma'am, something like that.
CHARLOTTE. The police must know how absurd that is.
WESTON. Oh, we do and we want to help you.
CHARLOTTE *(slowly, looking at Emily)*. I think I know who sent those letters, Mr. Weston. *(She stands.)* I'll talk to you tomorrow. I'll have the whole story for you by then.
WESTON. Oh, well, then, good night, Mrs. Wheeler. I'll look in about five, if that's convenient. Don't want to disturb the General.
CHARLOTTE. You're very thoughtful. Good night.
(Weston leaves the room. Roger and Ann go with him. The moment they are out of the room, Charlotte turns on Emily.)
CHARLOTTE *(furiously)*. *Now* are you satisfied?
EMILY. What do you mean?
CHARLOTTE. Even at the beginning I was suspicious, but I wouldn't let myself think such a thing. I couldn't believe

you would go so far, take such a revenge . . . accuse your own sister of murder.

EMILY. You're out of your mind!

CHARLOTTE. I'm not, but *you* are, with envy, with hate. You were jealous of John and me. You wanted him for yourself.

(Roger and Ann come back into the room. They are ignored as they listen.)

EMILY. That's enough, Charlotte!

CHARLOTTE. How you must have hated me . . . and what a fool I was not to have known you were in love with John even though he hardly knew *you* existed.

EMILY *(stung)*. That's not true.

CHARLOTTE. Of course it is! You've invented this whole thing. You pretended to yourself that John would have married you if I hadn't taken him away.

EMILY. He would have! I know it!

CHARLOTTE. But, Emily, he thought you were plain. He thought you were pitiable. He thought you were . . .

EMILY. Stop it! *(Charlotte turns away, Emily follows her.)* Now I'll tell you what I think, what I know; you married John to spite me, because I loved him. But you were prettier. You could charm men in a way I never could. John loved me first, long before you ever knew him.

CHARLOTTE. How can you say that?

EMILY. Because it's true. But, then, when he wanted to leave Concord, you wouldn't go.

CHARLOTTE. Everyone knows: it's all in your letters.

EMILY. They're not *my* letters, but whoever wrote them knows what we know.

CHARLOTTE. And what is that?

EMILY. That you killed your husband, Charlotte . . . you killed John. Heaven help you!

(Emily runs blindly from the room. Charlotte is stunned.)

ANN. Charlotte, Charlotte . . .

(Ann moves toward her, but Charlotte, as though hypnotized, walks past her.)

CHARLOTTE. I think I'll go to bed now. Good night, Ann . . . Dr. Waring.

(She leaves the room. Ann and Roger look at one another.)

ROGER. You . . . you think I ought to go and look after her?

ANN. No, not now.

ROGER *(tensely)*. It can't be true.

ANN. It's like a nightmare. Emily couldn't have said such a thing.

ROGER. And Charlotte couldn't have killed her husband . . . could she?

ANN. I don't know. I don't know.

Fade out.

Act Three

Fade in on General Bell in the drawing room. Roger is with him.

GENERAL. Can't breathe. Cold all the time. *This* room's like the North Pole. I'm catching pneumonia.

ROGER. But you haven't any temperature, General.

GENERAL *(irritably)*. I know when I'm sick, young man; I was sick before you were born.

ROGER. Yes, sir.

GENERAL. At my age, I can't take chances.

ROGER. I wanted to talk to you about Charlotte.

GENERAL. Charlotte? Thought you were marrying Ann.

ROGER. Well, yes, but I'm concerned about Charlotte . . .

GENERAL. Democrats going to nominate that Alton B. Parker. I feel it in my bones.

ROGER. I think Charlotte is almost . . .

GENERAL *(through him)*. Lucky thing for us, too, of course, if they . . .

ROGER. I want to talk to you about Charlotte, General.

GENERAL. And I don't. Do you understand? Want me to write it out for you?

ROGER. Then you know what's going on?

GENERAL. None of your business, whatever it is.

ROGER. But it's yours. Someone's accused your daughter of murdering her husband.

GENERAL. That fool thing on the mirror?

ROGER. Worse than that. They've gone to the police.

(The General at last is startled.)

GENERAL. You sure of this?

ROGER. A man from the Concord police was here last night.

GENERAL. I swear jealous women cause *all* this world's misery.

ROGER. You think it was Emily who told the police?

GENERAL. Who else would?

ROGER. Was she that jealous of her sister?

GENERAL. All her life, poor child.

ROGER. How was John Wheeler killed?

GENERAL *(slyly)*. You think maybe there's some truth in this?

ROGER. I don't know. General, did Charlotte and her husband ever quarrel about leaving Concord?

GENERAL. No. She worshiped him. Never could see why. I think he did want to try his luck in Boston, but he changed his mind. *(Shudders.)* Feel that wind? It's like a knife. Push me over to the fire and get Mrs. Wicks.

ROGER. Yes, sir. *(Roger rolls the General to the fire. Then he goes into hall as Emily enters from the front door.)* Oh, Miss Bell, I wanted to talk to you.

EMILY. Yes?

ROGER. It's about your sister, Charlotte.

EMILY. I'm afraid . . .

ROGER. That it's none of my business? Yes, I've heard that already.

EMILY. Then why do you insist on prying into our affairs?

ROGER. Because I want to help. Because I'm Mrs. Wheeler's doctor. Because I'm engaged to Ann.

EMILY. I can't help you. I'm sorry.

ROGER. You mean you won't?

EMILY. We are . . . private people, Dr. Waring.

ROGER. Miss Bell, where were you and your sister the afternoon her husband was killed?

(Emily gives him a long, venomous look; then she turns back into the hall and goes quickly upstairs. Roger goes into the dining room, where Ann is polishing silver.)

ROGER. Your father wants Mrs. Wicks.

ANN *(startled)*. Oh! Is Charlotte still asleep?

ROGER. She was, a half hour ago. I've been trying to talk to your father.

ANN. Not much help?

ROGER. None at all. He won't take this seriously. How did she sleep last night?

ANN. The same noises . . . the same nightmares.

ROGER. I should've given her a sedative. Where is Mrs. Wicks?

ANN. Upstairs.

ROGER. You know, I think I'm beginning to understand what happened. . . .

(There is a sudden scream from the second floor. Roger and Ann rush to the foot of the stairs.)

CHARLOTTE'S VOICE *(offstage)*. Leave me alone! Stop watching me!

(Charlotte appears at the head of the stairs, her hair

30

*disarranged, her face horrified. She looks back over her
shoulder as if afraid of someone behind her.)*

ANN. Charlotte, what's the matter?

*(Charlotte gasps as though struck from behind. She
reels, off balance; then falls. Roger catches her while
Emily and Mrs. Wicks appear at the top of the stairs.
Roger picks up Charlotte and carries her into the din-
ing room, where he places her on the table. Ann, Emily,
Mrs. Wicks, the General assemble.)*

ROGER *(to Ann).* Get my bag. It's in the hall. And some
water.

(Ann goes.)

MRS. WICKS. What happened, Doctor? I heard her scream
and then when I got to the landing, she'd fallen.

ROGER. I think she was pushed.

*(He works over Charlotte, who has begun to revive. Ann
returns with his bag and a glass of water, which she puts
on the table. Charlotte opens her eyes.)*

CHARLOTTE. She tried to kill me. She said she would. Just
like she killed John.

ROGER *(softly).* Who? Who is she?

CHARLOTTE. She's been watching me for years, waiting.
Every time I was happy she did something to ruin it.
Then she fell in love with John. But she couldn't have
him and she wouldn't let me have him. . . . Oh, stop
her, please *stop* her!

ROGER. Stop who? Charlotte, *who?* *(Charlotte begins to
twist convulsively on the table. Roger shakes her. Suddenly she is quiet, her face is odd, her eyes open.)* Who
wrote those letters?

CHARLOTTE. *I did.*

(Her voice is harsh, as it was at the beginning of Act Two. The others murmur with astonishment. Roger turns to Ann.)

ROGER. Get them all out of here.

(Ann pushes the General's wheelchair; Mrs. Wicks and Emily leave, reluctantly.)

ROGER *(to Charlotte)*. Why did you write those letters?

CHARLOTTE *(harsh voice)*. To punish her. *She* told you. I knew she would.

ROGER. Punish whom?

CHARLOTTE. Charlotte. She had everything. I had nothing. . . . It was always that way.

ROGER. Who are you?

CHARLOTTE. Janet. Oh, that's just like her. She never mentions my name. She's ashamed of me. *(Laughs.)*

ROGER. Have you known Charlotte long?

CHARLOTTE *(spitefully)*. All my life. I used to leave messages for her, but she never answered. She tried to ignore me, pretend I didn't exist. She shouldn't have done that.

ROGER. You were jealous of her?

CHARLOTTE. Of that weak creature? *(Sneers.)* No, but I despised her. She had everything. I had nothing.

ROGER. You killed John Wheeler?

CHARLOTTE *(gaily)*. Ask me no questions, I'll tell you no lies. . . .

(Roger shakes her. She twists convulsively.)

CHARLOTTE *(furious)*. She didn't deserve him. Why should she be happy? I wasn't. I killed him, but they'll think *she* did.

(She laughs hysterically. Roger gives her an injection. She grows calm. Ann enters from the hall.)

ANN. Roger, what's happening?

ROGER. Don't tell the others.

ANN. But what's wrong with her? Why did she say she wrote the letters?

ROGER. Because she did . . . part of her did.

ANN. I don't understand.

GENERAL'S VOICE *(from parlor)*. Ann? Where are you, girl?

ROGER *(quickly)*. She's two people.

ANN. Two people?

(Charlotte stirs on the couch. Roger crosses to her.)

ROGER *(to Ann)*. You'd better go to your father. Don't mention what's happened. I'll call you.

(Charlotte opens her eyes. Ann leaves the room.)

ROGER. Mrs. Wheeler?

CHARLOTTE *(wearily, herself again)*. Oh . . . Dr. Waring. *(Looks around, surprised.)* What am I doing here? Did . . . did I fall?

ROGER. On the stairs, yes.

CHARLOTTE. I seem to be your chief patient these days.

ROGER. Do you remember what happened to you on the stairs?

CHARLOTTE. No, not exactly. It's all so . . . oh, yes, I do remember. *(Suddenly tense.)* Someone was behind me. I couldn't see who it was. I thought it was Emily. I remember she said terrible things to me. Then I fell.

ROGER. It wasn't Emily.

CHARLOTTE. Not Emily? *(Puts hand to brow.)* I think something's gone wrong with my memory. I'm sure . . .

ROGER. Emily didn't write you those letters, Mrs. Wheeler.

33

CHARLOTTE. But if she didn't who did? No one else could except . . .

ROGER. Yourself.

CHARLOTTE. What are you saying?

ROGER. Listen to me carefully, Mrs. Wheeler, for your own sake. I had a hunch about this yesterday. Last night I reread a similar case. *(Slowly.)* You are two people.

CHARLOTTE *(bewildered). Two* people?

ROGER. The new word for it is split personality . . . an older word is possession.

CHARLOTTE. Possession . . . possessed by the devil. *(With wonder.)* I'm possessed?

ROGER. A few minutes ago you said your name was Janet. You said you hated Charlotte. You admitted writing those letters to yourself.

CHARLOTTE. I *can't* believe you! I'm not mad. I'm as sane as you. Oh, I know I'm often forgetful but I couldn't just . . . just *be* somebody else.

ROGER. Those times when you are forgetful, you're Janet. I began to suspect when you told me you couldn't remember what happened the afternoon your husband died, though you remembered the morning clearly.

CHARLOTTE *(slowly, with horror).* You mean I was . . . *someone else* the afternoon John died?

ROGER *(nods).* This is a terrible thing to say, Mrs. Wheeler, but you killed your husband.

CHARLOTTE. I don't believe you!

ROGER. The part of yourself called Janet . . .

CHARLOTTE. It's not true! It's not true!

ROGER. I wish it wasn't. Now, we haven't much time. The

police already suspect you of the murder. Worst of all, Janet is beginning to gain control of you.

CHARLOTTE *(not listening). I* killed John?

ROGER. We're going to have to fight Janet, you and I. This is a new problem for medicine. . . .

CHARLOTTE *(suddenly).* I'll go to the police. There's nothing else I can do.

ROGER. That wouldn't help matters. Remember they have no real proof you killed your husband. They know nothing about your . . . other self.

(Charlotte puts her hands to her face during this speech, apparently sobbing. As Roger finishes, she lowers her hands. She is smiling. She is Janet.)

CHARLOTTE. Poor Charlotte! *(Mimicks.)* I'll go to the police. *(Laughs.)* As if she'd dare. No, the police are going to come to her. I've seen to that.

ROGER. What have you done, Janet?

CHARLOTTE. Wait and see! I have a few surprises left.

ROGER *(fiercely).* What are you going to do?

(She laughs. Roger shakes her. She subsides, becoming Charlotte again, unaware of what's happened.)

CHARLOTTE. I feel so drowsy.

ROGER. Yes, I gave you a sedative. Mrs. Wheeler, I think we may be able to do something, but I'm not sure. No one knows much about this kind of thing.

CHARLOTTE *(shakes her head).* What can anyone do? I'm trapped. I still can't believe this is happening to me.

ROGER. But you suspected, didn't you? The other day when you said you thought someone was watching you . . .

CHARLOTTE. Someone *real*, not . . . not a devil, not a ghost, not something in me!

ROGER. I'm going to write Boston tonight for a specialist. They call them behaviorists.

CHARLOTTE. But what can they do for me? *I* . . . I killed John, my own husband. *I* killed him. And I can become this other person, just like that? Without knowing it?

ROGER. Without knowing it, or remembering what you've done. Now I'll get Mrs. Wicks. She'll put you to bed.

(He goes. She is still for a moment. Then, becoming Janet, sly and malicious, she crosses to hall mirror. Delightedly, she touches it, tracing MURDERESS *with her finger. Then she returns to dining room, opens black bag, removes a vial, pours its contents into the water glass; then she returns to the table, where she composes herself as Roger and Mrs. Wicks return.)*

ROGER. We must get her up to bed. Mrs. Wicks, will you stay with her at all times? You or Ann?

MRS. WICKS. Yes, Doctor.

ROGER *(taking box from bag)*. Give her one of these pills when she comes to. It'll relax her, and then . . .

(Charlotte moans and stirs. She opens her eyes.)

MRS. WICKS *(fearfully)*. Miss Charlotte?

CHARLOTTE. I feel so odd.

ROGER. It's all right, Mrs. Wheeler.

MRS. WICKS *(gives her pill)*. Take this, dear, you'll feel better. Then we'll tuck you in bed.

(Charlotte takes the pill and drinks the water from the poisoned glass. Then, with Mrs. Wicks's help, she stands up. Ann returns.)

CHARLOTTE *(smiling).* What a nuisance I've become!

ROGER. Don't you worry. Just get a good night's sleep. Then we'll have a long talk tomorrow.

CHARLOTTE. That will be nice.

(Charlotte and Mrs. Wicks leave the room.)

ROGER *(to Ann).* We'll have to declare her insane. It's the only thing we can do.

ANN. But, Roger, she isn't. You said she wasn't.

ROGER. If we don't, it means . . .

(There is a scream from Mrs. Wicks. Roger and Ann rush into the hallway. Emily is on the stairs. The General wheels into view. Charlotte lies on her back at the foot of the stairs, completely still. Mrs. Wicks stands over her, terrified. Roger, bag in hand, kneels down beside Charlotte and takes her pulse. Then he opens his bag and removes a stethoscope, which he places over Charlotte's heart while Mrs. Wicks talks.)

MRS. WICKS. Doctor, what's wrong? She said she couldn't breathe, said something was strangling her. Then she collapsed. She kept talking about Janet. Who is Janet?

ROGER. She was poisoned. But I don't see how she could've . . .

> *Then he finds the empty bottle in his bag.*
> *He holds it up, aware of what has happened.*

ANN. It was her other self, wasn't it?

> *Roger nods. As Mrs. Wicks weeps, Emily*
> *turns and goes upstairs. Fade out on figures*
> *on the stair.*

Dark Possession was the first play that I wrote for television. I remember asking a number of friends who were playwrights what on earth one wrote plays about. None was of much help except John Latouche, who promptly produced a magazine with a florid cover and read me aloud a description of the celebrated Beauchamps case . . . the first recorded case of schizophrenia in the United States.

The original Miss Beauchamps was inhabited by three selves, each of them quite independent of the other. Poor Miss Beauchamps had an especially difficult time with one of her selves who, whenever she took over, wafted Miss Beauchamps from her placid home in Boston to a restaurant in New Haven where she worked as a waitress. Fortunately she was saved by the behaviorist who later recorded the case. This took place at the turn of the century.

I used the general idea of the split personality, keeping it also in period; the result was melodrama and the play, although somewhat less than profound, still provides a sturdy vehicle for any good actress.

Geraldine Fitzgerald as Charlotte gave what is often recalled as one of the more exciting performances in television's brief history. Her shift from one self to the other was quite uncanny. I remember watching the kinescope of it with someone who said, "What remarkable make-up," not realizing that there had been no time for any physical change, that Miss Fitzgerald had transformed herself from within.

The mood of the play, as done on *Studio One* by Franklin Shaffner, was beautifully dark and strange. It has been repeated several times on television, most recently by Albert McCleery's *Matinee,* with Carol Stone. It betrays many of the beginner's faults, but for some lucky reason it plays like a dream. It is good melodrama without pretensions.

A Sense of Justice

Performed February 6, 1955
on
The Philco Television Playhouse (NBC)

Produced by Gordon Duff
Associate Producer: Robert Alan Aurther
Directed by Robert Mulligan

The Cast

PETER CHASE	John Hudson
DENNIS LEIGHTON	E. G. Marshall
HARRIS RHODES	Frank Overton
SALLY RHODES	Elizabeth Fraser
DORA RHODES	Sally Chamberlain
TED MURRAY	Paul Tripp
GUARD	Ed Walsh

Act One

Fade in on Peter Chase, a man of thirty, dark and average-looking. He is packing an overnight bag. On top of a shirt, he places a pile of magazines and newspapers. Photographs of one Dennis Leighton are prominent in all of them.

Close shot as he places his revolver in the bag and shuts it.

Dissolve to a railroad ticket booth as Peter Chase, bag in hand, wearing an overcoat, waits as the ticket seller checks his chart.

SELLER. Let's see . . . that's one hundred four, round trip to Talisman. . . . You want round trip, don't you? *(Peter shakes his head.)* It's cheaper in the long run. Well, that will be seventy-one sixty-seven including tax. *(Stamps ticket, takes Peter's money.)* That's quite a gambling town, I hear. Always wanted to go West myself, see the desert . . . nice dry climate. Here you go, son. *(He hands Peter the ticket.)* Don't gamble all your money away.

Dissolve to the barroom of the Paradise Casino in Talisman, a noisy, crowded place. It is early evening. The walls are lined with slot machines. Beyond the barroom we see a series of rooms set up for gambling. The customers are dressed in every conceivable fashion: some women are in evening dress, some men are in shirtsleeves.

Dennis Leighton, the owner, a pleasant man in his early forties, enters, his bodyguard close behind him. Smiling amiably, he walks the length of the room and goes into his office in the back.

Peter Chase, carrying a suitcase, enters; he looks about curiously; then he crosses to a telephone booth.

Dissolve to the hallway of Harris Rhodes's house. Rhodes is a man in his late thirties. His expression is both surprised and pleased as he hangs up the telephone.

Cut to adjacent living room, where his wife Sally, a blond Southern girl, his sister Dora, a plain woman not much younger than he, and Ted Murray, an elderly journalist, are all seated at a bridge table. Sally is shrieking with laughter at a remark of Ted's.

SALLY. Oh, Ted, you can't mean it! *(She glances toward hall as Rhodes enters.)* Who was that, Harris?
RHODES. Peter Chase. He's in Talisman.

SALLY. Now who on earth is Peter Chase?

DORA. He was in your company, wasn't he?

RHODES. That's right. *(To Sally.)* You remember. I've told you about him.

SALLY. I'm sure you have, Harris, but I can't keep them *all* straight. *(To Ted.)* The war's over ten years and they still keep coming. Sometimes I think Harris was in charge of the whole thing, the way he knew everybody.

TED. Harris is a born mixer, as we say.

SALLY. Isn't that the truth! People always take advantage of him. Harris, you remember that old master sergeant? The one who sent you the telegram from . . . where was it?

DORA *(to Harris)*. Wasn't he one of your lieutenants?

HARRIS *(nods)*. The best of the lot. *(To Sally.)* I invited him over.

SALLY. But, honey, he *isn't* going to stay?

HARRIS. Of course he is, if he wants to. We can put him up on the sofa.

SALLY. Dora, talk to your brother. I have no influence in my house.

DORA. Will he be here long?

HARRIS. Don't know. He didn't say what he was up to. Just said he was in town. *(He gets up from card table.)* We may as well break it up. He's on his way over now.

(Sally remains seated while the others put the table, chairs and cards away.)

TED. Where's he from? The East?

HARRIS. Concord, New Hampshire . . . a real Yankee.

SALLY. You know, not until I was a grown woman did I find out it was two words . . .

DORA *(dryly)*. We know your Confederate sympathies, Sally.

SALLY. Not sympathies . . . *values* is what we called them. People back in Greensboro had values when I was a girl. We had tradition.

TED. Well, you're a Westerner now, young lady.

SALLY. That may be, but I believe that certain things matter and the things that matter will *always* matter, East, West, North or South.

DORA *(to Harris)*. Did you ever hear from Peter Chase? I mean, before now?

SALLY *(gaily)*. No one listens to a word I say.

HARRIS. No, not often. He got married a few years back.

SALLY *(sudden recognition)*. Oh, he's the one we sent that yummy Meissen china to. How I wish I'd held on to that china. But I had no way of knowing it was Meissen until it was being wrapped up at the store and the man told me it was valuable. I found it in the attic in an old trunk. It was my mother's . . . she always had lovely things, but I never dreamed . . . *(Cautiously.)* I suppose he's perfectly *nice*, Harris.

HARRIS. Yes, perfectly nice, dear. Kind of studious, as I remember. I put him in for the Silver Star, but he never got it. Somebody lost the papers.

TED. Horrors of war, horrors of war. Sally, will you get an old man some bourbon and branch water?

SALLY. I certainly will, honey. *(She goes to console where there are glasses and bottles, mixes a drink.)*

46

DORA. Do you think he's here to gamble?

HARRIS. Not Pete. He didn't drink, didn't smoke, didn't run around . . .

SALLY. My, he sounds like the most interesting man!

DORA. He just has values, Sally.

SALLY. You can have values and enjoy life . . . in moderation.

(The doorbell rings. Harris crosses to door, goes into hall. We can hear his voice and Peter's.)

SALLY. I wish the Army hadn't been so big.

HARRIS *(offstage).* Come on in, Pete, and meet the folks.

(Harris and Peter enter. Sally rushes forward effusively. Dora and Ted rise. Pete shakes hands all around as he is introduced.)

HARRIS. My wife Sally, Pete Chase. My sister Dora. And this is Ted Murray, our local publisher; writes everything that's fit to be written.

TED. It's a small paper. How do you do?

PETER. Hello.

SALLY. I've heard so much about you, Mr. Chase. Harris here talks about you all the time, and the war . . . why, I think I know that old war backwards.

HARRIS. That's pretty much the way we fought it. Sit down, Pete. I'll get you a drink. How's your wife? She stay back in Concord?

PETER. She's dead. *(An awkward silence. Grave faces are adjusted uneasily. Peter, sensing this, is less abrupt.)* It . . . it was an accident. . . .

(But both Harris and Sally have spoken at the same time.)

SALLY. Oh, honey, how awful for you . . . ⎫
HARRIS. I'm sorry I didn't . . . I'll get ⎬ *(Together.)*
that drink. ⎭

TED. Well, young man, you come West to make your fortune?

PETER. No, sir. I just came West.

TED. You'll like it. I did. I swagger around like an old frontiersman, but I came from Scranton originally. Came out when I was your age.

SALLY. And he's done so well. Haven't you, Ted? With the paper and everything. Ted's the smartest man we know, Mr. Chase.

TED. I expect I am at that, Sally.

SALLY. You should see all his books. He reads, reads, reads, morning, noon and night.

HARRIS. So does Dora.

SALLY *(flatly)*. It's different with Dora. She's a librarian.

TED. Dora, play something for us.

SALLY. Yes, Dora, do! She plays the piano like an angel, Mr. Chase. I took violin for five years as a child but I'm afraid I wasn't very musical. My poor mother was so disappointed. She played the guitar.
(Dora, who has been watching Peter with some interest and sympathy, goes to piano. Ted and Sally follow her. Peter and Harris sit together at the other end of the room. Dora starts to play Chopin.)

SALLY. Oh, honey, not that! Play something we can all *sing*.
(Dora shifts to Victor Herbert. Dora and Ted sing softly an off-key duet, "Ah, Sweet Mystery of Life," in the background while Harris and Peter talk in the foreground.)

HARRIS. It's good to see you, Pete.

PETER. Good to see you, Rock.

HARRIS. Rock! I haven't heard that name in ten years. I guess I was the only guy named Rhodes in this country who wasn't called Dusty.

PETER *(smiles)*. No, you were Rocky Rhodes.

HARRIS. The war seems like a hundred years ago.

PETER. I think about it sometimes. I . . . I liked a lot of it.

HARRIS. Not me.

PETER. Well, things were simpler then. We knew where we stood.

HARRIS. Gosh, I'm sorry about your wife.

PETER. You would have liked her. We were in an accident. Car hit us. I was battered up a bit and she was killed, last February . . . February 14, St. Valentine's Day.

HARRIS. No kids?

PETER. No, nothing.

HARRIS. Are you still with that . . . what was it? Insurance?

PETER. Real estate. No, I quit. I quit this month.

HARRIS. Going to retire?

PETER *(smiles)*. I might, now you mention it.

HARRIS. Well, if you have no other plans, Pete, why don't you settle down here? You could come into the business with me.

PETER. You make this offer to all graduates of Company C?

HARRIS. No, just to the best officer in Company C.

SALLY *(from piano)*. You wouldn't like something to eat, would you, Mr. Chase? Or some coffee?

PETER. No. No, thank you. I had dinner. Nice place you got here, Rock. You must be doing pretty well.

HARRIS. Big things happening out here.

PETER. So I've heard. I've read a great deal about a man named Leighton. According to the papers, he owns most of your state.

HARRIS. Yes, he's a big man out here. You're going to stay with us, aren't you?

PETER. Well, I hadn't planned . . .

HARRIS. Of course you will . . . long as you like.

SALLY (*suddenly*). Harris, I smell smoke.

HARRIS. You always smell smoke, Sally.

SALLY. And there's always something burning. I better look in the kitchen. I'm always leaving that old oven on.

TED. You got his vote yet?

PETER. Vote?

HARRIS (*laughs*). That's right. I'm running for the state legislature this fall.

PETER. Just like you said you would. We always thought you'd be a Senator.

TED. Over my dead body, he'll be.

HARRIS (*quickly*). Ted and I don't see eye to eye on things.

TED. I'll say we don't. I like this boy, Pete. I like him a lot. When he came back home I was going to put him on a horse with silver armor and I was going to send this boy of mine into battle. . . .

HARRIS (*softly*). Lay off, Ted.

TED. Going to send him into battle. So what does he do? Well, he goes into battle all right. He gets himself a Sherman tank instead of a horse and he goes in on the wrong side. If I didn't love you like a son, Harris, I'd . . .

HARRIS. Come on, Ted. Pete doesn't want to hear politics.

PETER. But I do. What side *did* you take, Harris?

TED. He took the safe one. He got Dennis Leighton to back him and now he's Dennis Leighton's man. I suppose you've heard that name — Talisman's one big celebrity.

PETER *(nods)*. Yes. He's the boss of the state, isn't he?

TED. Pretty near. The boss of the county, anyway, and the biggest gambler in Talisman. Every dead man they ever fished out of the Blue River was acquainted with him.

HARRIS. You know there's no proof. He's ruthless, maybe, but he's not a killer.

TED. You read my paper tomorrow morning. I've got some names. Some dates. Some facts.

(Sally returns.)

SALLY. The oven was off but I still smell smoke. *(Tense silence.)* What's everybody so solemn about? Oh, Ted, you've been talking politics to Harris. That's not fair. If Mr. Leighton wants to groom Harris for Congress, *I say fine.* Harris will be a good Congressman. You have to admit, except for those awful gambling places, we were never in the news until Mr. Leighton came along, and all publicity's good publicity as long as they spell your name right.

PETER. I've read a lot about Leighton.

TED. I guess everybody has. He's not just *our* scandal any more. He belongs to the whole country now.

(The fire whistle sounds in the distance.)

TED. Sally's right: there *is* a fire.

HARRIS. That's a house fire on the south side.

TED. We'd better go. *(To Peter.)* The volunteer firemen's

51

clarion call to duty! Nice to meet you, Mr. Chase. You coming, Harris?

HARRIS. Yeah. Excuse us, Pete . . . be back soon as we can.

(Harris goes to the door, accompanied by Sally.)

SALLY. Didn't I tell you there was smoke? Now, Ted, you hurry back when that old fire's put out. We'll be here.

> *Dissolve to Leighton's office at the Paradise Casino. It is an austere, businesslike office, not at all like the gaudy nightclub. Leighton is alone. He is reading a newspaper, his expression amused. Headline says* BOSS CONNECTED WITH '51 KILLING. *There is a picture of him on the front page. A knock at the door. Bodyguard enters, a Western type, plump, Stetsoned. Rimless glasses, however, remind us the West isn't what it was.*

GUARD. All taken care of, Mr. Leighton.

LEIGHTON. Anybody see you?

GUARD. Nobody. Went up in smoke so quick . . . it was a real pretty job, if I say so myself.

LEIGHTON. Good scout! *(Rises.)* I'll be over at Harris Rhodes's if anybody wants me.

> *Camera follows him as he leaves his office and walks the length of the barroom. Dissolve to the Rhodes's terrace. Sally, Dora and Peter are looking out into the night. Every now and then, far off, we hear fire engines.*

SALLY. My, look at that! Why, that fire must be three miles away and you can see the flames so clear. *(Sighs.)* You all want some coffee? I'm going to make some. *(She goes inside.)*

DORA *(after a pause)*. It must be strange to visit an old friend after all these years.

PETER. The Rock . . . I mean, your brother's changed.

DORA. A little? Or very much?

PETER. Very much. I've always looked up to him. Rocky Rhodes was our portable saint. Once he . . . but you don't want to hear about all that.

DORA. I don't *mind* hearing about the war.

PETER. But you'd rather not. It's a dull subject, unless you were there.

DORA *(smiles)*. Yes, it's a dull subject. I don't like the past.

PETER. And I don't like the future. *(Beat.)* You know, when I first saw the Rock tonight I didn't recognize him: his face has changed.

DORA. Faces do.

PETER. Ten years ago everybody was twenty. Now we're thirty.

DORA. Harris is thirty-seven.

PETER. Something happens in the face.

DORA. Lines? Age?

PETER. No . . . it's softness. Something's happened to him. It's like . . . something that was once very clear has become blurred.

DORA *(gently)*. You are too severe.

PETER. Well, I've changed too.

DORA. Is there so much virtue in being twenty all your life?

PETER *(not listening)*. It's like being a sieve, with your life all leaking away and nothing done and a lot lost. *(Pause.)* I'm sorry. I didn't hear your name.

DORA *(smiles)*. Dora. An old-fashioned name . . . if you like the past.

PETER. I like Dora.

DORA. Not many men like "Dora."

PETER. You're not married?

DORA *(shakes her head)*. And not apt to be. For a long time I said no and then, after a while, it wasn't necessary to say no. *(Looks off.)* Why, there's Harris.
(Harris enters. He is grim.)

DORA. What is it . . . what happened?

SALLY *(entering)*. Oh, good, you're home early. We stood outside and watched that fire for a while. I didn't expect you for hours.

HARRIS *(slowly)*. It was Ted. It was Ted's house that burned down.

SALLY. Ted! Oh, that poor man! How on earth did it happen?

HARRIS. I don't know. Ted has a crazy notion Mr. Leighton's men did it.

SALLY. That's ridiculous!

DORA. I *know* they did!

HARRIS. This was just a fire. An accident. Houses catch fire every day.

SALLY. They certainly do. And I hope Ted was properly insured; if he was, it's a blessing in disguise because that place of his was the ugliest house in town, and those old frame houses are perfect tinder boxes . . . give me ce-

54

ment block any day; it's not as pretty, maybe, but it's safe. Harris, did you renew *our* fire policy?

DORA. Mr. Leighton isn't apt to burn down this house.

HARRIS. Don't talk like that!

SALLY (*sweetly*). Mr. Leighton is our friend, Dora, and Ted is our friend and when friends don't like each other, well, the thing to do is stay neutral. You just end up with nobody liking you if you start to take sides.

DORA. Yes, we must avoid being disliked.

SALLY. I'm not sure I like your supercilious tone, Dora.

DORA. Does it offend you?

SALLY (*viciously*). You should remember that you're not the Queen of England going around with a crown on your head and feeling better than everybody else because of reading those dumb books and not being married like every other normal person. . . .

HARRIS. Shut up, Sally!

SALLY. I will not be dictated to. Dora has no interest in your future but *I* have. I don't want you to be just a small tradesman all your life. I want you to be a great man . . . a man of substance people look up to and say, "Isn't that Mrs. Rhodes the luckiest woman, being married to such a man?"

(*During this Leighton has entered from the terrace and stands, unobserved, listening.*)

LEIGHTON. Atta girl, Sally!

(*They all turn, startled.*)

HARRIS. Oh, Mr. Leighton, I didn't expect you tonight.

LEIGHTON. Just passing by.

SALLY. My, you slid in here so quiet. You nearly gave me

heart failure. Sit down over there and let me get you something to drink. Oh, and this is Mr. Chase, all the way from the state of New Hampshire, where they have nothing but snow. . . .

LEIGHTON *(shaking Peter's hand)*. Welcome to Talisman.

(Peter stares at him, fascinated.)

SALLY. What'll you drink, Mr. Leighton?

LEIGHTON. A bit of bourbon . . . and a dash of branch water.

SALLY *(going onto terrace)*. I used to think when I was a child that the snow must be sweet like sugar because it was so white. We didn't have snow in Greensboro.

LEIGHTON *(crossing into room)*. Good evening, Dora.

DORA. Good evening, Mr. Leighton. Have you been to see the fire?

LEIGHTON. No.

HARRIS *(quickly)*. I meant to call you this afternoon about the campaign.

(Sally gives Leighton a drink.)

LEIGHTON. Thank you, Sally. *(To Harris.)* To you. It now looks like you'll be nominated right off, on the first ballot.

SALLY. Isn't that the most thrilling thing? Harris, you're going to be a state senator!

DORA. But *then* what will he do?

SALLY. What do you mean what will he do? He'll get ready to go to Washington next.

LEIGHTON. He'll be representing the good people of Talisman, Dora.

DORA. All the people?

LEIGHTON. All the *good* people.

PETER. At least the ones who voted for him.

LEIGHTON *(chuckles)*. That's right. Practical politics.

PETER. And Harris will have to be practical, if he wants to get elected.

LEIGHTON. I'm sure we can count on him . . . he's a pretty solid fellow, old Harris.

(Fire engine screams past the house. All pause.)

HARRIS. Ted was here tonight.

LEIGHTON. Oh. *(Pause.)* You trying to win over the opposition?

HARRIS. He's an old friend.

LEIGHTON. I like Ted too.

HARRIS. But he takes things too seriously sometimes.

LEIGHTON *(offhand)*. Well, that's the way you build up circulation.

SALLY. I must say you're being a perfect Christian. If I were you, I'd be furious at those awful things he writes about you, Mr. Leighton. I just don't know *why* he does it.

LEIGHTON. I don't know why either.

PETER. Don't you think he's being paid off?

LEIGHTON *(nods)*. I'm sure Ted has his price like any other man.

DORA. Perhaps he does it as a public service.

SALLY. Public nuisance, you mean.

LEIGHTON. Well, you can't please everybody.

HARRIS. I was there with Ted at the fire.

LEIGHTON. He take it pretty hard?

SALLY. I'd smelled smoke, oh, a long time before the fire engines. . . . I'm like that, I can smell smoke a mile away, but nobody else ever does. . . .

LEIGHTON. Poor Ted didn't have the house insured.

HARRIS. Are you sure?

LEIGHTON. I have an interest in the insurance office. Ted forget to keep up his payments. The policy lapsed this month.

SALLY. Isn't that awful! But I must say he brought it on himself; that's the first thing we always pay, Harris and I.

LEIGHTON. Ted's careless. He always lets loose ends lie about, doesn't he, Harris?

HARRIS. I guess you're right.

DORA *(to Harris)*. I thought you admired Ted.

HARRIS. Well, I do . . . of course. . . .

LEIGHTON *(blandly)*. We all admire crusaders.

DORA *(to Harris)*. Remember after the war, the plan you and he had to close the gambling houses?

LEIGHTON *(chuckles)*. I never knew that. Why, Harris, you surprise me.

HARRIS. It was . . . it was just an idea. I mean . . .

SALLY *(sharply)*. Just an idea of Dora's.

HARRIS. I didn't know so much then about Talisman. . . . Ted and I are just friends.

LEIGHTON. According to Ted, I'm a national scandal.

PETER. The bigger the scandal the better the business.

LEIGHTON *(pleased)*. Just what I was going to say. You hear of me back East?

PETER. Yes.

LEIGHTON. You read about the wicked gambling halls and here you are . . . on business?

PETER *(softly)*. Yes, on business.

(Ted enters, grim; there is a fierce moment as he and Leighton face one another; neither prepared for this meeting.)

LEIGHTON. Sorry to hear the news, Ted.

TED. The whole house is gone. We got there too late to save my cats. I had three Siamese cats. One of them was nine years old.

LEIGHTON. That's tough luck.

TED. You're slipping, Dennis. First you start by killing men and now you're killing Siamese cats. Better watch out: you may end by stealing nickels.

LEIGHTON. I'm sorry . . . about your cats.

TED. It's a funny feeling to go out of the house you've lived in twenty years and come back to a cellar full of ashes.

LEIGHTON. You seem to be having a run of bad luck.

TED. You read this morning's paper, didn't you?

HARRIS. Have something to drink, Ted.

TED. Leighton, how far can a man go?

LEIGHTON. As far as he likes.

TED. He can go right out of this world, can't he?

LEIGHTON *(nods)*. Right out of this world.

TED. No one can stop him?

LEIGHTON. Maybe. Maybe not.

TED. And there's no justice, is there?

LEIGHTON. Only what you make. Only people.

TED. You burned down my house.

LEIGHTON *(carefully)*. No, it was the fire burned down your house.

TED. And you killed my three cats. . . . Were you so afraid of me? Was I getting too close to you?

LEIGHTON. But you *are* close to me. We're both on the Main Street of Talisman.

TED. Well, I'm not afraid of you, Dennis.

LEIGHTON. Should you be?

TED. And I mean to send you to prison.

LEIGHTON. Good luck.

TED. You don't own all the state or all the country yet.

LEIGHTON. I'm not in a buyer's market.

HARRIS. Ted, I wish you'd . . .

SALLY *(giggling nervously)*. Goodness, how grim you all are! I haven't the faintest notion what you men are carrying on about.

HARRIS. I wish . . .

SALLY *(fiercely)*. Harris, be still . . . keep out of this.

TED. Good night . . . friends. *(He turns and goes.)*

LEIGHTON. I never saw a man who was so enthusiastic about cats.

DORA. Is that the moral you wish us to learn, Mr. Leighton?

LEIGHTON. The moral? No, this is a story with no moral. Here we are . . . that's all. Just trying to get by. *(To Harris.)* We can talk tomorrow about the primary. Good night, Sally, Harris . . . Dora.

SALLY. I'll see you out, Mr. Leighton. *(They cross onto terrace.)* You must excuse Ted . . . he's never like this, but, after all, it's a real shock losing your house, and those awful cats.

LEIGHTON *(pausing)*. Good night, Mr. Chase.

PETER. Good night, Mr. Leighton.

LEIGHTON. Drop by and see me if you have the time . . . Paradise Casino, on the Main Street.

PETER. I will.

LEIGHTON. He mustn't get the wrong impression of us . . . eh, Sally?

SALLY. I should say not. . . . Cats and birds I just hate . . . they feel so odd; birds feel odd, I mean. My brother made me hold a canary once and, you know, I screamed, those feathers and that funny shivering. . . . Now you promise me you'll come to dinner soon.

LEIGHTON. It's a promise.

(He goes. Peter starts to follow, but Sally turns and takes his arm.)

SALLY. You come back on in, honey, and we'll have a little drink to relax us all, after this craziness.

(They enter the living room and pause, startled, as Dora turns on Harris.)

DORA. You are the weakest man I have ever known.

HARRIS. Dora!

DORA. Ted was your friend.

HARRIS. What could *I* do? Build him another house?

DORA. You stood there and took the side of a man who's a murderer, a . . .

HARRIS. There's no proof. How do we know he set fire to the house?

DORA. You know and I know it and, the worst thing of all, Leighton knows *we* know. Oh, how he loved it! Watching you squirm, watching you crawl . . . !

(Dora runs from the room.)

SALLY. My hands are shaking so! All this excitement. I think I'll go up to bed. *(To Peter.)* I must say this is an *unusual* welcome to Talisman; things aren't always so peculiar here. Now I'll just fix up the sofa for you and in the morning . . .

PETER. That's all right. I'll be staying at the hotel.

SALLY. Oh. Well, if you prefer, of course. . . . Good night, you'll come to supper tomorrow anyway. *(Goes to Harris, kisses him.)* Come up to bed soon, honey. You look so tired, poor lamb.

(She goes. The two men are left alone. There is a long pause.)

HARRIS. We seem to be deserted. I wish you'd stay here.

PETER. I can't. *(He puts on his coat.)*

HARRIS *(defensive)*. You *have* to compromise.

PETER. Sure . . . sure.

HARRIS. It's not like it was, not like the war: everything was simple then. A man knew what he had to do.

PETER. But the war's over, isn't it, Rock?

HARRIS. It's over and a man has to compromise a bit, here and there.

PETER. He set fire to the house, didn't he? *(Harris only gestures miserably.)* Well, I'm glad I got a chance to see Leighton like this. It's made the thing I'm going to do a lot easier.

HARRIS. Made what a lot easier? What're you going to do?

PETER. I'm going to kill him . . . tonight.

(Peter goes, slamming the front door after him.)

Fade out on Harris's stunned face.

Act Two

*Fade in on the bar of the Paradise Casino
as Peter enters, looks around, crosses to bar.
Cut to the Rhodeses' living room. Dora
and Harris are struggling with Sally over the
telephone.*

SALLY. Harris, if you don't let me use that phone I'll run
out in the street like this, I swear I will.

DORA. Don't let her, Harris.

SALLY. You keep out of this. *(Pleads.)* Honey, *please* let me
call Mr. Leighton before this awful man kills him.

HARRIS. No.

SALLY. You mean you'll just stand by . . .

HARRIS. No, I'm not going to stand by. I'm going down to
the Casino. I'm going to talk to Pete. I'm going to stop
him.

DORA. I'll go with you.

HARRIS. No.

DORA. It'll take me a second to change. *(She leaves room.)*

SALLY. What good will talk do with a crazy man?

HARRIS. Pete's not crazy.

SALLY. I suppose now he's just as sane as you and me, com-

63

ing all the way across the country to kill Mr. Leighton when he doesn't even know him.

HARRIS. I don't know why he wants to kill him, but I'm going to find out.

SALLY. Harris, don't be a fool. Keep out of this. Let me call Mr. Leighton. He can handle the whole thing and you won't be mixed up in it. Harris, please . . . please.

HARRIS *(grimly)*. No. If Leighton finds out . . .

SALLY. Nothing will happen, exactly.

HARRIS. If he finds out he'll take care of Pete.

SALLY *(exploding)*. You and your precious Pete! Here he comes out of nowhere, a wild-eyed maniac . . . no, don't say he isn't; I can tell by the look in his eye; he's insane and Mr. Leighton will have him put away, that's all. They'll give him some tests or something at the hospital; that's all they'll do, honey. He's sick, the boy's sick.

HARRIS. We don't know. We don't know what he has against Leighton. That's what I've got to find out.

SALLY. And while you're finding out, he's gone and shot our best friend in this town.

HARRIS *(softly)*. Our best friend in this town?

SALLY *(pleading)*. Oh, honey, don't be angry with me. I'm thinking about you all the time. You're all I have in the world. I'd do anything for you: I'd go out and beg on the street corner, I'd steal, I'd . . .

HARRIS *(embraces her)*. Sally, Sally, let me do this my way. Trust me.

SALLY. I trust you, Harris, but you've a soft heart. I have to be tough for both of us. Honey, *your* chance is now, with Mr. Leighton. Nothing must happen to him until you're in the legislature.

HARRIS. You think it will do me good, belonging to a gangster?

SALLY. You don't belong to anybody. Once we get what we want, we can *be* what we want.

HARRIS. It's not that easy. When a man owns you, you can't just up and say thanks and so long.

SALLY. You're not turning against him?

(Harris does not answer, has no answer.)

SALLY *(threatening).* Because if you do, I'll . . .

HARRIS. Sally, you've got to understand. I feel responsible for Pete.

SALLY. Even if Mr. Leighton's lying dead in a pool of blood at the Paradise Casino?

HARRIS. He's not that easily killed. *(Starts to door.)* I'm going now. I don't want you to call anybody. You promise?

SALLY. No.

HARRIS. Sally, do you love me? *(Sally kisses him.)* Promise me you won't touch that phone till I get back.

SALLY. I promise.

HARRIS. Good girl. *(Kisses her.)* Don't worry now. Nothing's going to happen to anybody tonight.

He starts to go as we dissolve to the barroom of the Paradise Casino. Leighton's bodyguard is sitting at the bar. Peter sits now at a table. Surreptitiously, he checks his revolver.

Harris enters the bar and crosses to Peter

just as the phone rings and the bodyguard goes to answer it.

Cut to the Rhodeses' living room. Sally is on the telephone.

SALLY. You must find Mr. Leighton. It's urgent. A matter of life and death, yes, yes, yes, this is Mrs. Rhodes. Well, when do you expect him? . . . All right, listen to me carefully. Tell him the man he met tonight — he'll know who I mean — is a . . . a gunman, yes, a hired killer from the East. Of course I'm serious . . . don't be a . . . now, listen: tell him I think this man is going to wait for him at the Casino tonight. . . .

(Dora, fully dressed, enters during this. She tries to stop Sally, who manages to finish before Dora can break the connection.)

DORA. Harris told you not to.

SALLY. So he lets people get the better of him. He's sentimental about that awful war and the people he knew.

DORA. No one can say *you're* sentimental about anything.

SALLY. That's your opinion. Anyway I've saved Mr. Leighton.

DORA. Sally, you are wonderful!

SALLY *(a martyr)*. Make fun of me, I don't mind, but I make allowances because you're nothing but a pathetic old maid who's never going to have a man to marry. . . .

(Dora deliberately strikes Sally across the face. Sally gasps and recoils.)

DORA. I'm sorry, Sally. I shouldn't have done that. It gave me too much pleasure. *(She turns abruptly and leaves.)*

*Dissolve to the barroom. Harris and Pete
are talking intently in front of a slot machine.*

HARRIS. That's not the reason.

PETER. O.K. It's not the reason.

HARRIS. You don't come all the way here because you didn't like what you read about Mr. Leighton.

PETER. But here I am.

HARRIS. Sally was going to call Leighton. She was going to tell him everything.

PETER *(nods)*. That was a mistake, my telling you.

HARRIS. I wish you'd think this thing over.

PETER. But I have. Every day now for a year.

HARRIS. Since your wife died?

PETER *(nods)*. Since she died and I lost interest in a lot of things.

HARRIS. I wish you'd see a doctor or somebody who'd . . .

PETER *(grins)*. I only broke some ribs in the accident. I wasn't knocked on the head.

HARRIS. I didn't mean it that way. . . .

PETER. You think I'm a candidate for Section Eight? Well, a lot of people may think I am before the night's over. Look, Leighton's going to be here any minute. Go on home, Rock.

HARRIS. Pete, I could stop you. I could stop you myself.

PETER. How?

HARRIS. I could call the police.

PETER. And I'd deny everything.

HARRIS. I could tell Leighton.

PETER. There won't be time.

HARRIS. I could stop you with my bare hands.

PETER. We won't have a brawl because I've got a gun in my pocket and I'd shoot first.

HARRIS. You'd kill *me?*

PETER. I wouldn't want to.

HARRIS. We were friends.

PETER. That's right.

HARRIS. But not any more?

PETER. Not tonight. And there won't be any tomorrow for me, so that takes care of us, Rock.

HARRIS. Then tell me why, just tell me that.

PETER. I want to kill him, that's all.

HARRIS. That isn't all. People don't do things like this.

PETER. Rock, don't . . . don't interfere.

HARRIS. He's not as bad as you think. *(Quickly.)* He's got a lot of good qualities. He . . . he gave the new hospital to the town, paid for it himself.

PETER. You've changed, Rock.

HARRIS. Well, so have you.

PETER. You used to be more . . . definite.

HARRIS. All right, so I'm not a brave free soul flapping in the wind . . .

PETER. No, you're not a brave free soul . . .

HARRIS. I never was.

PETER. *I* thought you were. That's what counts, what people felt you were. We all felt the Rock would never let us down.

(During this Peter sees Leighton as he enters the barroom with three men. Peter pulls the gun from his pocket. Harris grabs his hand and holds it; in a moment, Leighton is gone. No one has seen this struggle.)

PETER. I could kill you!

HARRIS. Go ahead.

(Peter shoves past him toward Leighton's office. Harris stops him as the bodyguard appears from the far end of the bar.)

GUARD. Evening, Mr. Rhodes.

HARRIS *(distracted)*. Oh, hello.

GUARD. I got a call from your wife tonight. Or at least some woman who said she was your wife.

HARRIS. Yes?

GUARD. She said there was a guy coming here tonight to kill Mr. Leighton, said Mr. Leighton would know who it was because he met the guy at your house. It was all pretty wild.

HARRIS. I'll say. You see, my wife . . . well, she's kind of nervous. You know how women get. . . .

GUARD. Sure. I figured it was a joke or something.

HARRIS. I wouldn't worry Mr. Leighton with it.

GUARD. I won't. Anyway, he's got the message in his office.

HARRIS. You mean he knows?

GUARD. Well, sure. I wrote down all she said. That's my job. He'll get a good laugh out of it.

HARRIS. Yes . . . yes. I guess he will. Tell him she's having one of her nervous nights.

GUARD. Sure.

(The guard walks off. Harris turns to Peter.)

HARRIS. *Now* will you quit?

(Dora has entered. She joins them.)

DORA *(to Harris)*. Sally . . .

HARRIS. Telephoned. I know. Mr. Leighton's got the message.

Cut to Leighton in his office. He is on the telephone. Three men are casually examining papers. Leighton is talking as the guard enters.

LEIGHTON *(into phone).* You say the lieutenant governor's out of the state? *(Guard hands him message, which he glances at while he talks.)* No, no, I won't. Betty, get me the governor. I know it's two in the morning. Wake him up. *(He hangs up, looks at the message again. Guard whispers something to him. Leighton looks surprised. The guard goes.)* Now, gentlemen, to business.

Cut to the bar.

HARRIS. He's been warned. They won't let you near him.
PETER. Then I'll wait till he comes out.
DORA. Harris, let me talk to him, please.
(She crosses to Peter; Harris follows.)
DORA *(to Harris).* Please.

Harris goes to bar. Dora follows Peter to a booth. She sits beside him as he turns and faces the door to Leighton's office, waiting.

DORA *(softly).* Why are you doing this?
PETER. Because somebody must do it.
DORA. Yes, but why you?
PETER. Because I want to.
DORA. Is that a reason?
PETER. It's enough reason for me.

DORA. You won't tell me why . . .

PETER *(he turns to her, looks at her for the first time)*. Look, for the past year back in Concord I got up every morning at eight o'clock. I lived in a boardinghouse. I read the same newspaper every morning and I rode the same bus to work. I got to the office and the receptionist made the same joke to me she'd made ever since I came to work the year I left the Army. Then I saw the same people and did the same things and said the same things I've done and said for ten years, and when the day was over I'd go back to the boardinghouse and go to sleep just so I could start that day all over again . . . doing nothing all over again. And it seems it's always been that way, except for the Army.

DORA. Your wife . . .

PETER *(nods)*. I loved her and she's dead. I'm not holding a wake because I lost one person. Death never bothered me. I saw a soldier — friend of mine — bleed to death in a German garden and you know what I thought? The only thing I could think was: His blood's the same red the flowers are.

DORA. Your own life's over if you do this thing.

PETER. I know it.

DORA. And you don't care?

PETER. No.

DORA *(suddenly sharp)*. You know, you sound as if you were the only one who'd discovered life was stupid. Of course it's stupid but *you* needn't be. You have yourself. Do you think I enjoy being what Sally calls a conceited old maid? Do you think *I'm* deliriously happy stamping books in that library? No, I'm not, but I live because it's the only thing I have to do, and I hope.

PETER. I hope, too. I hope I'll be able to kill Leighton. That will be one thing done. One good thing.

DORA *(softly)*. Is there *anything* I can say or do to stop you?

PETER. Yes. *(Suddenly passionate.)* Yes, you can say, "Life is wonderful; justice is done." You can say the reception-ist will have a different joke every morning and that the bus I ride to work will find a new route each day. . . . You can promise me I won't grow old and stupid like all the world I see . . . old and stupid and alone. Promise me that and I'll stay right here.

DORA. I would give you all that if I could.

PETER *(touched)*. If you could . . .

(The bodyguard approaches.)

GUARD. Your name Chase?

PETER. That's right. *(He gets to his feet.)*

GUARD. Mr. Leighton wants to see you, in his office.

DORA *(frightened)*. Peter!

(Harris hurries over.)

DORA. Leighton's sent for him.

HARRIS *(quickly)*. Ask Mr. Leighton to come out here. I'm sure he . . .

GUARD *(grimly)*. He wants to see him inside.

DORA. Peter . . . don't go.

(Peter smiles at Dora, then he goes to the office. Harris and Dora look at one another as we fade out.)

Act Three

Fade in on Leighton's office. He is still in conference with the three men, one of whom is the Attorney General of the state. Papers are spread out on the desk. Guard enters.

GUARD. The gentleman from the East is outside.

LEIGHTON *(to men)*. Will you excuse me? Just take a second.

ATTORNEY GENERAL. It's getting late, Dennis.

LEIGHTON. I know, but we've got to wait for that call, anyway. Would you mind stepping outside?
(The three men leave the office.)

LEIGHTON *(to guard)*. Tell him to come in.
(Guard goes out, returns with Peter, who stands in the center of the room. Guard leaves.)

LEIGHTON *(abruptly)*. I understand you want to kill me. That right? Well, go ahead. . . . What's the matter? Just press the trigger in your pocket. Couldn't be simpler.

PETER. You *want* me to kill you?

LEIGHTON. It's not what I want. It's what *you* want, or what somebody wants. Who hired you?

PETER. Nobody.

LEIGHTON. Ted in on this?

73

PETER. No.

LEIGHTON. Harris know?

PETER. Yes, he tried to stop me.

LEIGHTON *(thoughtfully)*. You don't look like the sort any-body would hire for a job like this.

PETER. I wasn't hired.

LEIGHTON. Oh? Then did I ever . . . well, *do* anything to you?

PETER. No.

LEIGHTON. To a member of your family, maybe? Or a friend?

PETER. Yes, to Harris. You bought him.

LEIGHTON. He didn't have to sell. . . . So you haven't been hired. I've never done anything to you or to anybody you know, yet you came all the way West to kill me.

PETER. That's right. All the way West. . . .

(A beat. Peter's hand is in his coat pocket. In the silence we hear the click of the safety being thrown.)

LEIGHTON. You know you'll be arrested. . . .

PETER. I know.

LEIGHTON *(sighs)*. Then you're a lunatic and this is fame. Lunatics usually kill a President or at least a governor. I should be flattered.

PETER. I think I'm sane.

LEIGHTON. I'd hate to see your idea of insanity.

PETER. You figured when I came in here I wouldn't do any-thing, knowing there were people around. I ought to tell you: I don't plan to escape.

LEIGHTON. Why have you picked me?

PETER. Because you deserve it.

74

LEIGHTON. More than most people?

PETER. Much more.

LEIGHTON. How do you know?

PETER. I've read everything there is to read about you.

LEIGHTON. Ah, but those are only newspapers. No one believes them.

PETER. Even if only half of what they say is true you deserve this.

LEIGHTON (*slowly*). You think I'm that bad?

PETER. Tonight you burned down a man's house . . .

LEIGHTON. Self-defense. He was trying to ruin me.

PETER. And you're a murderer, too.

LEIGHTON. How can you be sure? You still haven't told me *why* you feel you're the one to judge and execute me.

PETER. No one else would.

LEIGHTON. Is that the only reason?

PETER. Have you never heard of a disinterested act?

LEIGHTON. But it's not disinterested. You don't want to live. You're too much a coward to kill yourself so you make up your mind to kill a wicked stranger and then go to your reward in the electric chair. Of course you are interested. You want your justice at my expense. Look, boy, there are people like me as long as there are people.

PETER. And every now and then there is one like me.

LEIGHTON (*sighs*). No, no. It's true that I live outside the law. That's my way. But it's not yours. You are a moral man. You can't do this. I can, but not you. If you want to destroy me personally, then do it Ted's way. Ted's effective.

PETER. Is he?

75

LEIGHTON. You know, the trouble with you conscientious men is you think too simply. Tear down the gambling hall and there'll be no gambling. Kill the boss of the state and the state is free. But it will do no good your killing me. There'll just be a new boss of Talisman tomorrow. Some other Dennis Leighton.

PETER. I know what's right.

LEIGHTON. Do you? Do you really?

PETER *(tensely)*. Don't talk.

LEIGHTON. Afraid to kill a man while he's talking?

PETER. You're not going to talk me out of it.

LEIGHTON. Look, boy, you've got this . . . this justice of yours on the brain.

PETER *(with difficulty)*. Sometime, somewhere a man should act, just once in his life, even at the end.

LEIGHTON *(carefully)*. Then listen to me. I am all that you've ever heard of me. Does that give you confidence? I've done all the things you read about in the papers. Now! That ought to make it easy to touch that little bit of metal . . . but before you do, think of this town, these people. I'm one of them. They made me. There were gambling halls and murders before me and I expect they'll go on a long time after me. They created me, boy, I didn't create them. I've lived the only way I knew to live. It may seem strange to you back there in some old quiet town in the East where you do things differently though you do the same things.

PETER. What're you trying to prove?

LEIGHTON. Prove! I'm *telling* you what you ought to know already. Let the state do justice, if it can.

PETER. The state belongs to you.

LEIGHTON *(dryly)*. Not quite. Look, son, suppose this really worked, suppose you became a kind of hero, the one person to kill a man he didn't know, just out of a sense of justice, what would it prove? Everyone has a sense of justice and in most cases it's self-interest. If they took what you did seriously you'd have them all tumbling against each other like so many dominoes. No, the law may be weak; the law may be for sale; but it's better than this other thing. Believe me. Stay alive, son. It takes more nerve. I know. *(Leighton turns in his chair, his back to Peter. He talks, half to himself.)* You know, when I was a boy I lived on a ranch. Almost the first thing I remember was buzzards gathering over the dead livestock. We went broke, my family went broke when the ranch just turned to dust one day. All the springs dried up. The cattle died and those buzzards got fatter and fatter. . . . And now they're collecting tonight . . . this time for me. Well, it's been a good life . . . for me. *(Leighton turns about. Peter has left the room. His gun is on the desk. Telephone rings. Leighton reaches for it. For the first time we see that he has been handcuffed all through this scene, unknown to Peter.)*

LEIGHTON *(into phone)*. You get the governor? Oh, I see . . . the governor can't be reached.

(He puts the receiver down. He reaches for the revolver. The door opens. The three men have returned. The Attorney General takes the gun from him.)

LEIGHTON *(rising)*. Well, I suppose it's time to go.

Leighton, with a man on either side and one in front, walks jauntily through the door and down the length of the bar. At the door, he meets Ted, who has just entered. Leighton pauses. Through the window we can see Peter, Harris and Dora, waiting outside in in the street.

Ted and Leighton look at one another. Grimly, Ted hands him a copy of a special newspaper edition. The headline: LEIGHTON INDICTED FOR MURDER.

Leighton drops the paper coolly and goes out. Ted follows him.

Leighton, accompanied by his arrestors, walks slowly past Peter, Harris and Dora, as we fade out.

This play was a strange experience for me. It was my first attempt at political — in the more exact sense of the word — statement, and I committed many of the errors I've often criticized in others: I was imprecise and not entirely honest. The play was written during the last act of the Senator McCarthy drama and though I never saw in him anything more sinister than a gaudy buffoon, his case had, I believed, reillumined an ancient debate: should one act directly and kill the serpent in the egg? Should one ignore the law to save the law? I rather think now that Peter

Chase should have killed Leighton. But unfortunately when writing villains, one tends to identify with them: after all, what are they but reckless men who indulge in reality that which the rest of us experience only in guilty dreams, in reluctant nightmares?

Leighton finally dissuaded Peter Chase from killing him with but one argument: you are not disinterested, you want justice at my expense. To my mind the logic of that was intellectually — if not dramatically — sufficient, incontrovertible. But in making this point, I gave Leighton altogether too great an awareness of his own position . . . such men, it has been my experience (limited, certainly, but intense), are seldom that reflective. And of course the final argument is too perfunctory.

The main criticism to the play was, I think, valid: Peter Chase was too shadowy; many felt his obsession to be incredible. To that argument I can only beg the audience's indulgence: there is so little time on television in which to show one's characters and I had, as well as my protagonist, Leighton, Harris, Sally, Dora, Ted all bursting to be born. Though one might safely quarrel with the dramaturgy, with the philosophic resolution, the characters were oddly alive. Elizabeth Fraser in particular gave a stunning performance as Sally: an adoring wife, a silly woman, a shrewd schemer, giddily Southern, all these at once. E. G. Marshall, as Leighton, was as sharp and precise as a razor. I have worked with him three times, in *Barn Burning,* in *Smoke* and in *A Sense of Justice.* Without exception, he is the strongest actor I know. Robert Mulligan directed with his usual clarity and inventiveness . . . the handcuffs at the end were his idea and worth a dozen speeches.

A few months after the play was produced on television, the Playhouse decided to repeat it, with a different cast. They were ready to start rehearsal when the advertising agency involved abruptly forbade the production: too controversial. What was possible in February, 1955, was no longer possible in August, 1955.

Summer Pavilion

Performed May 2, 1955
on
Studio One (CBS)

Produced by Felix Jackson
Directed by Paul Nickell

The Cast

THERESA CARTER DURAND	Miriam Hopkins
FATHER DURAND	Joe Sweeney
BELLE TRAVERS	Ruth White
HELEN DURAND	Elizabeth Montgomery
WINTER CARRINGTON	Wyatt Cooper
NED WELCH	Charles Drake
MRS. CARRINGTON	Carol Veazey

Act One

*Fade in on the drawing room of the Du-
rand house in Audubon Park, New Orleans.
The house is early nineteenth century. The
room is spacious, Georgian: tall windows,
Adam fireplace, no rugs over parquet floors
and, here and there in the large room, an oc-
casional piece of furniture: Sheraton, Hep-
plewhite. Through sliding doors, the front
hall connects with the drawing room. From
nearby, in sporadic bursts, there is a sound
of riveting.*

*Theresa Durand, a handsome lady of mid-
dle age, descends the stairs, carrying a bunch
of placards in one hand and a feather duster
in the other. We follow her as she enters
drawing room. Her father-in-law Durand, an
elderly man, sits by the window, reading. He
does not look up as she enters.*

MRS. DURAND. A glorious morning! A heavenly day!
*(He merely nods, still reading. She does not wait for an
answer. Instead she moves about the room, dusting carefully, almost gaily, until, arriving at a particularly fine*

83

*console, she pauses and then, with a grim expression, she
sets one of the placards on it and we move in for a close
shot of the sign, which reads:* FOR SALE $1500.)

MRS. DURAND. Where is Belle?

DURAND. Upstairs, dusting her phonograph records.

MRS. DURAND. She cares for those records as though they
were rare porcelain . . . I get so tired of them I could
scream. Not that I have anything against music in general. *(Raises voice.)* Belle! Belle honey! You come on
down here. *(To Durand.)* She knows it's her turn to look
after the tourists.

BELLE'S VOICE *(off stage).* Comin', Theresa . . .

*(Mrs. Durand busies about the room, placing price tags
on all the furniture.)*

MRS. DURAND. I have never minded being the doer in this
family, but there are limits to my strength.

DURAND. There are no limits to your strength.

MRS. DURAND. Is that meant to be irony, Father Durand?

DURAND. No, no, my dear. We would all starve without you
to look after us.

MRS. DURAND. We shall all starve anyway if we don't sell
some more of the furniture: the lovely, lovely furniture.
Oh, it breaks my heart to see it go, all bundled up, piece
by piece and spirited away to dreary middle-class
homes. . . .

DURAND. Considering the prices you get, the homes can't be
too middle-class.

MRS. DURAND. You know what I mean: *nouveaux* . . .
nouveaux riches, who buy our furniture, thinking they
can buy what we are, but they can't, never, never!

(Pause.) I wonder if I'm asking enough for that Sheraton sofa.

DURAND. Are dealers coming today?

MRS. DURAND *(nods).* A Mr. Wingo of Baton Rouge is coming all the way down the river to look at that sofa. He is what they call an interior decorator — such a nice voice he had over the phone — and he's doing up a house and he wants only fine things, he says, so we must receive him graciously. . . .

(Belle enters, a fragile, defeated woman of early middle age.)

MRS. DURAND. There you are, Belle darling. I've nearly finished, as you see, but I never mind a little light labor; a little work has never hurt anyone, though the hands suffer perhaps. *(Holds them up sadly.)* How white they were! Remember, Father? Remember when I married your son and the *Times Picayune* said, "The bride, Miss Theresa Ann Carter of Biloxi, wore her great-grandmother's veil of Brussels lace and her complexion was like moonlight on a camellia." *(Laughs.)* That's what it said, it really did . . . a bit high-flown maybe, but those were gallant days, and my hands *were* lovely too, much my best feature. And *now* look at them, I ask you! Look what's become of them!

DURAND. Just liver spots, Theresa. Nothing serious. I was younger than you when I got them.

MRS. DURAND. Father Durand! Liver spots! *(Turns to Belle.)* Belle, I want you particularly to be pleasant today because an important interior decorator — how people can allow someone else to arrange their homes I shall never comprehend — this man is coming here, and don't be shy with him; remember who you are, you're Miss Belle Durand of Audubon Park and he's just like a servant.

BELLE. You mean I am Belle Travers, of Chicago.

MRS. DURAND. What did I hear you say? What name? Have my ears betrayed me? Has that awful riveting become so loud I no longer hear properly?

BELLE. I am not an old maid, Theresa. I am a married woman and my name happens to be Travers.

MRS. DURAND. I am aware of your mistake. But I thought we had agreed not to refer to it, to act as if you had never eloped with an undesirable only to be deserted in Chicago, left in the lurch, as the saying goes. . . .

DURAND. Theresa, be kind.

MRS. DURAND. Kind! I am downright indulgent! I received Belle with open arms when she returned, and to this day I have never once said "I told you so!" . . . now have I, Belle? Admit it: I have never said "I told you so" . . . no, not once. *(Looks to window.)* Oh, that riveting will drive me mad! Father, call them up again. Tell them who you are. Tell them they must work more quietly in Audubon Park. *(Crosses to window.)* That hideous great hole where all our gardens were . . .

DURAND. The building looks as if it might be handsome when it's done.

(Belle finishes arranging price tag.)

MRS. DURAND. No modern building, no housing project can be an improvement on our gardens. *(To Belle.)* Belle honey, place the price tags a little less discreetly. We mustn't hide our light under a bushel, and it saves that awful haggling if they know we mean business.

DURAND *(softly quotes)*. "The woods decay, the woods decay and fall, and after many a summer dies the swan."

MRS. DURAND. I hate swans. They have ugly dispositions. Belle, is Helen awake? Did you call her?

BELLE *(nods)*. I took coffee to her just now.

MRS. DURAND. My poor little girl, slaving away at that school. Perhaps if we sell enough furniture she could take a year off and . . . no, no, she must learn to struggle like the rest of us.

DURAND. I never struggle.

MRS. DURAND. No, Father Durand, you cannot be accused of contributing to our support or to the betterment of the world. You simply read while Rome burns.

BELLE. This *is* Father's house, Theresa, and we are living from the sale of his furniture.

MRS. DURAND. I suppose I am not to be considered a member of the Durand family. It's true I only married into it a mere thirty years ago, married into this lofty family descended from French pirates . . .
(Helen enters. She is a pretty girl, very like her mother, though unaware of the similarity.)

MRS. DURAND. Helen, my baby, you're going to be late for work.

HELEN. No, Mother, I don't have to be at the school till eleven. Good morning, Grandfather.

DURAND. Good morning, Helen.
(Mrs. Durand crosses again to window.)

MRS. DURAND. You must continue to make a good impres-

sion at the school. Your honorarium just barely supports
you here, my baby. Oh, who'd've dreamed the money
would all have faded so fast! It seemed such a lot when
I married your father. . . . My poor gazebo looks so
sad and lonely out there with all that mess around it.
Father, what *did* you say to them yesterday?

DURAND. I said the gazebo was two hundred years old and
must be preserved as a permanent treasure of the state
of Louisiana. I told them it was a small building but a
perfect one.

MRS. DURAND. What did they say to that?

DURAND. They said they were going to tear it down.

MRS. DURAND. I knew you'd blunder! I should've gone to
see them myself.

HELEN. But after all, Mother, it's now their property.

MRS. DURAND. But it *was* ours. Morally it is ours though
they may own the land beneath it. Father, you must
telephone the governor.

DURAND. The governor?

MRS. DURAND. His aunt was a Pardoe and they are cousins
of my mother's. He'll understand. He'll stop those vandals. Oh! That noise! I tell you it will drive me insane.
Well, since you refuse to act, I will appeal to the governor on my knees . . . I shall throw myself on his
mercy . . . *(Stops.)* Was that the doorbell? Quick now,
Father, go to your room.

DURAND. I shall go in town to the library.

MRS. DURAND. Your eyes will fall out from reading one day.

DURAND. Too late . . . even for that. I'm afraid you will
put me in my coffin, eyes and all.

MRS. DURAND *(shudders).* Don't speak of death to me.

DURAND. Why not? I am nearly eighty and you are nearly sixty.

MRS. DURAND. It turns my blood cold to hear you talk of death.

DURAND. My blood *is* cooling, Daughter. *(At door.)* I shall be home for supper. *(He goes.)*

MRS. DURAND. A wasted life! Reading and thinking and nothing to show for it, nothing done. *(Pause.)* I guess no one was at the door.

HELEN. He has been happy.

MRS. DURAND *(fine contempt).* Oh, *that!*

BELLE. Which rooms do you want me to show today?

MRS. DURAND. All the ones down here and the front bedrooms upstairs. And don't forget the story about Jefferson Davis when he stayed here and the butler lost his boots . . . that's always amusing and it's historic. . . . I'm going up to lie down now. *(Starts upstairs.)* Call me when that interior-decorator man is here, the one from Baton Rouge. He'll want only the sofa, but we must try to interest him in that hideous maple bed upstairs, the one nobody wants. And, Belle, do look pleasant; you might even try to smile every now and then; it creates a nicer atmosphere. After all, life's not so bad, is it, honey? Helen, don't you be late for the school.

(She goes. Belle looks after her grimly. Helen crosses to window.)

HELEN. I wonder why Mother is so upset because the gazebo is going down. She almost never went near it before the land was sold.

BELLE. Your mother doesn't like to let go of anything. . . . Is Winter coming to supper tonight?

HELEN *(flatly).* I suppose so. It's Friday. He always comes on Friday.

BELLE. You do like Winter, don't you?

HELEN. Of course I like him. It's just . . . well, he's Winter. I've known him so long . . . too long, I guess, to be romantic.

BELLE. But you must marry him. It's the thing to do. You can be a June bride. I wish I'd been one, all married in a church . . . instead of at the city hall before catching a bus to Chicago. It never does to be impulsive. Don't be like me.

HELEN. No, I won't be like you. You were honest. You were in love. I'm not and that's the difference between us, Aunt Belle.

BELLE. Don't talk of love, baby, never talk of love. I know. Marry wisely. Marry a boy they'll approve of . . . like Winter. Don't get them down on you . . . ever! They are merciless when you make a mistake.

HELEN. Sometimes I think I would like to make a mistake, a really splendid one!

BELLE. I did and where did it lead? To a hotel room, unpaid for, in Chicago, on the coldest winter day in the history of that city. I remember reading about the weather in the paper while I waited for my husband to come back. I read that paper through five times, very carefully, before I realized I'd never see him again. Then I packed and came home.

HELEN. Poor Aunt Belle!

BELLE. Not poor! I had two weeks before he left me. Those fourteen days are my secret capital.

HELEN. Two weeks. . . . I envy you.

BELLE. Envy me! Oh, no, my dear. You can't envy me when you'll have a lifetime with Winter, away from here, away from this sad house. . . .

HELEN. Sad house?

BELLE. The saddest I have ever known, for us at least. . . . They never let us alone; not for one minute are we alone here.

HELEN. You mean the family . . . ?

BELLE. I mean the ghosts, Helen, the ghosts! They are in every room of this house, reminding us we belong to them. . . .

HELEN (smiles). But they're *our* ghosts. That's a comfort.

BELLE (slowly). *Our* ghosts, yes, that's the strangest part of all. Helen, there are times when I believe . . . I know it sounds crazy, but there are times when I believe *we* are the ghosts and don't know it, that we're the dead and the others, the ones I see sometimes standing lonely on the stairs or looking back at me through old mirrors, are really the living, and they've forgotten us. . . .

MRS. DURAND'S VOICE (offstage). Belle! Belle! Can you come up here a moment?

BELLE. Watch the door, Helen. I'll be right back.

(She goes. Helen turns as doorbell rings. She crosses to hall as the front door opens and Ned Welch enters. He is thirty and vigorously handsome.)

NED. I guess we're the first customers of the day.

HELEN. Oh . . . yes.

91

NED. I've always wanted to see the inside of this house. *(He goes into living room.)* Say, where's all the furniture?

HELEN *(following).* Some has been sold.

NED *(looks at tag).* Oh, I see. Everything's for sale. I guess the Durands are pretty hard up.

HELEN. Yes, very hard up.

NED. What do we do? Just look around on our own?

HELEN. Well, I think . . .

NED. Wonderful proportions. Say, an Adam fireplace.

HELEN. You're not from New Orleans?

NED. No, I'm from Chicago. I've only been here a few weeks. I'm on a job and I've been meaning to see the inside of this house ever since I got here. . . . They certainly built to last, didn't they?

HELEN. Yes, they built to last. I'm afraid the brick may outlast the family.

NED. Do you know the Durands?

HELEN. Yes, I'm Helen Durand.

NED. Oh . . . oh! I didn't say anything wrong, did I?

HELEN *(smiles).* You were discreet.

NED. In a way, we're neighbors. Did you know that?

HELEN. Why, no. Are you staying with . . . with the Carlisles?

NED. No, I'm in charge of the housing project. I'm a construction engineer . . . Welch, Ned Welch.

HELEN. How do you do?

NED. You know, I've seen a good many old houses, but this is the first time I've seen one where the family which built it still lives in it; you know, just the way their ancestors did.

HELEN. I'm afraid we don't live *quite* the way our ancestors did. We're broke. We live on tourists, and the sale of furniture.

NED *(still looking about)*. I guess this is what they mean by tradition.

HELEN. Do you enjoy building?

NED. It's a living. . . . Yes, I like it. By the way, I'm sorry we had to tear up those gardens of yours. They went with this house, didn't they?

(Mrs. Durand enters, beaming.)

MRS. DURAND. I thought I heard voices. I'm so pleased you've come to see us. . . . I'm Mrs. Durand and I bid you welcome. Was it a nice drive?

NED. I'm afraid . . .

MRS. DURAND. I love the river road, though in the old days we used to travel by steamer. Now: this is the sofa. It was bought by Emil Durand in 1760. He was mayor of New Orleans and it's still in perfect condition to this day. The upholstery is nice and I wouldn't change it if I were you. A lovely piece for any home, even a modern one. Oh, the cleverness it must take, Mr. Wingo, to decorate someone else's house tastefully! My hat is off to you, sir, and, by the by, I don't know how you are for beds, but we happen to have a lovely one up-stairs . . .

HELEN. Mother, he's *not* the interior decorator.

MRS. DURAND. But I thought you said he . . .

NED. My name's Welch, Mrs. Durand. I think I've seen you before, out back. You see, I'm in charge of the housing project.

MRS. DURAND *(freezing)*. Oh. I see. We . . . we are aware

of your presence, of course. It would be difficult *not* to be aware!

NED. It's an awful racket, I know. Be patient with us.

MRS. DURAND. Of course some might say it was vandalism, but not I . . . *I* try to understand. I don't mean to throw myself in the path of progress. I realize only too well the old order changeth. . . . However, wanton destruction of the rare and the lovely hurts me to the quick.

NED. Destruction? Of what?

MRS. DURAND. I am referring to the gazebo in the garden, which has been marked by you for demolition.

NED. You mean that old cabin with the roof gone?

MRS. DURAND. I mean the pavilion where, as a young bride, I used to sit on summer nights, watching the moon rise over this house.

NED. Well, it spoils the approach to the project.

MRS. DURAND. So we have been told.

HELEN. Mother, I've got to fly.

NED. I'd better go too.

MRS. DURAND *(coldly)*. The admittance fee is one dollar. You may leave the money on the hall console as you go out.

(Helen and Ned cross to hall. Mrs. Durand remains in the drawing room.)

NED. I guess I'm in enemy territory.

HELEN. She doesn't mean to be rude.

NED. Where are you off to?

HELEN. I teach at Miss Haskins's Seminary for Young Ladies.

NED. Pretty grim?

HELEN. Yes, pretty grim.

NED. Do you go out much?

HELEN. Sometimes, when I'm invited. I've got to catch my bus.

NED. Have dinner with me tonight. I haven't been out once since I came here. Nothing but work.

HELEN. Well, I don't believe . . .

NED. After all, I'm a neighbor. A barbarian in need of civilizing . . .

HELEN. I don't think that.

NED. I'll pick you up at seven.

HELEN. No, no, I can't. I'm sorry, but . . .

MRS. DURAND'S VOICE *(offstage)*. Has he gone yet, Helen? *(Helen and Ned exchange a conspiratorial glance.)*

HELEN. Yes, Mother, he has. *(To Ned, whispering.)* I'll meet you after dinner, at Ronsard's . . . it's in the Old Quarter!

MRS. DURAND'S VOICE *(offstage)*. Vandals, vandals, that's what they are! Coming down here, destroying what we cherish, what they can't appreciate!

> *Dissolve on this speech to drawing room. We come in on Mrs. Durand, who is talking to Winter Carrington, a soft, doe-eyed Southern youth, who listens appreciatively. Helen sits opposite them, her eyes on the clock, which says nine. She fidgets uncomfortably. At the opposite end of the room, Durand sits, reading comfortably. A sad ballad of the twenties is being played on an old-fashioned victrola, the possession of Belle.*

MRS. DURAND. Vandals, that's what they are, Winter, van-dals! And to think I mistook him for an interior decora-tor and told him all about the sofa before Helen saw fit to enlighten me. I could have bit my tongue off with shame.

(Belle collects emptied coffee cups. She is in and out during this scene, changing records, winding the phono-graph.)

WINTER. I must say, Mrs. Durand, you have the courage of a lioness to face commercial people without flinch-ing.

MRS. DURAND. We come of tough stock, Winter. When we lost everything in the war, my mother took in laundry for two years. My sainted mother did other people's laundry. . . . Of course it was mostly flat work, but even so, a lady!

WINTER. You are a worthy descendant. Mother always says Theresa Carter Durand is the bravest and least com-plaining woman in Audubon Park.

MRS. DURAND. Well, it's nice to be appreciated. One likes to know that others feel . . . Helen, will you stop fidget-ing!

HELEN. Was I fidgeting?

MRS. DURAND. You were. If our company bores you, I sug-gest you and Winter go to the movies.

WINTER. Would you like that, Helen? There's a double fea-ture at the Royal.

HELEN. I don't think so, Winter . . . thank you.

MRS. DURAND. Aren't you playing the phonograph a little loud, Belle? *(Belle turns it down.)* That's much better.

I tell you, Winter, the art of conversation in America has declined along with everything else. . . .

DURAND *(suddenly)*. There never was any art of conversation in America.

MRS. DURAND *(gaily)*. Go back to your book, Father Durand, back to your book! *You* are the worst offender!

DURAND. Literature is my Great Wall of China. Behind it I cower, waiting for the Mongols.

MRS. DURAND. Whatever *that* may mean.

WINTER. My mother had a mongrel once. It was an unusually clever dog, black and white, something like a wolfhound.

MRS. DURAND. They say that mongrels are clever, but I'm not convinced, and speaking of mongrels, Helen, did that young man from the North make any mention of my campaign to save the gazebo?

HELEN. What? Oh, no, he didn't, Mother.

MRS. DURAND. Helen, you have been watching the clock for the past half hour. Have you an appointment?

HELEN *(suddenly rising)*. Yes, Mother, I have.
(All eyes are upon her.)

WINTER. But, Helen honey, this is Friday, we always go to the picture show Friday.

MRS. DURAND. And where do you think you are going this time of night?

HELEN. To see a friend, Mother. I promised.

MRS. DURAND. Are we to be vouchsafed the name of this mysterious friend?

HELEN. No, Mother, you're not.
(An ominous silence. Belle laughs nervously.)

MRS. DURAND. What is so amusing, Belle?

BELLE. I'm sorry, Theresa. I was just thinking of something.

MRS. DURAND *(grimly)*. So was I. Helen, you have never gone out before without telling us *where* you were going.

(Helen crosses to door.)

HELEN. Good night, Mother. I'll be home early. Good night, Winter.

(Mrs. Durand starts after her.)

WINTER. But, Helen, this is Friday night . . .

DURAND. I think that fact has been clearly established. *(To Helen.)* Have a good time, darling.

HELEN. Thank you, Grandfather.

(She goes out. Mrs. Durand follows her into the hall.)

MRS. DURAND. Helen baby, is anything wrong?

HELEN. No, Mother.

MRS. DURAND. But then where are you going? Whom are you seeing? Baby, this is your mother who's asking you.

HELEN. To see a friend . . . don't you trust me?

MRS. DURAND. Of course I do, angel. . . .

HELEN. I'm a grown woman and I am going out to see a friend.

MRS. DURAND. Then if that's the way you feel, very well, I can't stop you. I am only your mother who loves you.

HELEN. Good night, Mother.

*She goes, closing door behind her, as we
fade out on Mrs. Durand's startled face.*

Act Two

Fade in on Ronsard's, a picturesque bar in the Vieux Carré with candles on the tables, stone walls and a clientele evenly divided between the odd and the ordinary. There is dancing and the jukebox music is sentimental. Ned is alone at a table when Helen enters.

NED. I thought you'd stood me up.

HELEN. I'm sorry. I couldn't get away sooner.

NED. I'll bet your mother doesn't know you're seeing me.

HELEN. No, she doesn't.

(They sit down.)

NED. I'm glad you're here.

HELEN. So am I.

NED. It's quite a place . . . lot of characters. I guess they're all artists.

HELEN. I don't think so. I'm told the artists wear neckties and the tourists wear blue jeans.

NED. Do you come here often?

HELEN. I've never been here before.

NED *(surprised)*. But . . . well, didn't you suggest . . .

HELEN *(laughs)*. Yes, I did. I've always wanted to come, but

99

since the family disapproves, there was never anyone to take me.

NED. Then we're both tourists.

HELEN. That's right. I like it, don't you?

NED. Very much.

(An elderly waiter comes over.)

WAITER. What's your pleasure?

HELEN. I should like some Pernod. It's supposed to have wormwood in it and according to my mother it will drive you mad.

NED. I'll have it, too.

(Waiter goes.)

HELEN. How depraved we are! I wish Mother could see me now.

NED. Must we talk about . . . Mother?

HELEN. No, never again. *(Laughs.)* I do talk about her a lot, don't I? We all do. I suppose it's because she has such . . . such charm. No, she really does. She's not always so awful.

NED. You were never going to talk about Mother again.

HELEN. You tell me about *your* mother. That's fair.

NED. I don't have one. No family at all.

HELEN. I'm sorry.

NED. I'm not. . . . That's a beautiful house you live in.

HELEN. Well, I'm afraid we are eating it, room by room. We live on the sale of furniture, and not much else. . . .

NED. But *you* work, don't you?

HELEN. Oh yes, I'm the only one who does. You see, as a rule, our family doesn't work. I don't know why, but they just don't.

NED. Somebody must've done *something* to get things started.

HELEN. We were pirates in the eighteenth century. We stole.

(Waiter returns with two Pernods.)

NED. Then here's to piracy!

HELEN. On the high seas. *(Beat.)* I *am* glad I went out with the first stranger ever to ask me.

NED. You don't go out very much, do you?

HELEN. Not like this. I mean . . . *(Laughs.)* I've done nothing but talk about myself, and Mother says no girl can be popular if she talks about herself to a man. Girls must listen.

NED. I like listening to your voice. It's very soft, very quiet.

HELEN. And yours is a growl. *(Quickly.)* Which I like of course. Have you enjoyed New Orleans?

NED. I guess it's what they call gracious, but the tempo's too slow for me.

(There is a sudden pause. Both are embarrassed, tense, expectant. Both speak at once.)

HELEN. It's chilly in here, don't you think?
NED. I wish they'd open a window or some- } *(Together.)*
thing.

(They laugh.)

HELEN *(holds glass to light)*. What an odd color it is . . . like a tiger's eye.

NED. Shall we talk about tigers?

HELEN. Yes, tigers and lions and leopards. We shall never run out of conversation.

NED. No, I don't think we will.

Dissolve to the same scene later. They are dancing. Both are more intimate, less strange, with one another.

HELEN. . . . and he's a clerk in a law office. Winter's been a clerk for ten years and maybe he won't be anything else.

NED. You don't love him, do you?

HELEN. No, no, I don't. But I wish I did because of the family. It would make Mother so happy if I were to marry Winter.

NED. That's not much reason, is it?

HELEN. No, I don't suppose it is.

NED. If anybody back home heard somebody was getting married to please their family they'd drop dead.

HELEN. It is old-fashioned, isn't it?

NED. Yes, very old-fashioned. You know, I'd like to get a bulldozer down here and tear right through the center of Audubon Park just to see what would happen.

HELEN. But so much of it's worth keeping . . . some of it's so lovely.

Cut to the door of the bar. Winter enters, disconsolate. Waiter greets him cordially.

WAITER. Hi there, Winter. Haven't seen you in a long time.

WINTER. Mother's been sick.

(Winter has seen Ned and Helen. He crosses to them grimly.)

WINTER. Well, Helen, I had no idea you were a patroness of this place.

HELEN (*startled . . . embarrassed*). Oh! Winter, this . . . this is Mr. Welch.

NED. Pleased to meet you. Helen was just . . .

WINTER. I don't think Mrs. Durand would approve of Ronsard's.

HELEN. It's not half as bad as she thinks.

NED. Pull up a chair, Winter.

WINTER. No, thank you. Helen, you must go home. Your mother's very worried.

NED. Miss Durand had a date with me.

WINTER. Miss Durand is my fiancée.

NED. So?

HELEN (*quickly*). I'd better go. Good-by, Ned. Thank you.

NED. But it's early. I thought we . . .

HELEN. I can't help it. . . .

WINTER. I'll see you home, Helen.

(He takes her by the arm and leads her to the door. They leave. Waiter crosses to Ned.)

WAITER. Isn't Mr. Carrington and the lady going to stay?

NED. No, they're not staying.

WAITER. Anything wrong, sir?

NED. No, everything's just swell. (*Stands up abruptly.*) How much?

Dissolve out on his angry face to the Durand drawing room. Mrs. Durand is in midtirade. Father Durand listens impassively. Helen is angry but submissive.

MRS. DURAND. . . . and with our enemy too! Oh, don't say he's not an enemy, because he is. He's everything that wants to destroy us body and soul and the gazebo. That's what he is, a destroyer.

HELEN. Mother, he's not. He's a perfectly nice young man.

MRS. DURAND. Nice! Does a nice young man take you to a den of artists and worse?

HELEN. I took him.

MRS. DURAND. Don't try to defend him. I know about places like that one . . . I know what goes on when those people with beards get together.

HELEN. Oh, Mother, really!

MRS. DURAND. Not to mention going out with a man on first meeting . . .

(Telephone rings in the hall. Helen starts for it but her mother is there first.)

MRS. DURAND. Hello. Yes? Who is calling her? Oh, Mr. Welch. This is Mrs. Durand. We met this morning. Helen has asked me to say that she doesn't feel she should see you again. . . . You know she is engaged to be married and down here engagements are looked upon as very, very serious matters. Yes, I understand. No, she won't come to the phone. No, I wouldn't suggest calling her tomorrow. I . . . why, he hung up! The rudeness!

HELEN *(furious)*. You had no right to speak for me.

MRS. DURAND. I am your mother.

HELEN. How could you lie to him?

MRS. DURAND. You are engaged, Helen, that is a fact, not a lie.

HELEN. You mean I'm trapped in this house.

MRS. DURAND. Trapped? The doors are unlocked . . .

HELEN. I warn you, Mother, if you ever again interfere I'll . . . I'll . . .

MRS. DURAND. What? What will you do? Go to Chicago and marry a prize fighter? Is that what you'll do? Is that what Belle has advised you to do? Because if she has, be warned: you won't be able to come back. Do you hear? We won't take you.

DURAND (*softly*). Theresa, that's enough.

MRS. DURAND. Enough, is it? Enough that I want to save her from misery and disaster? We are not fit for the world of the vandals . . . any more than they are fit for us. We must stick together with our own kind and that's what Helen will do and that's why she'll marry Winter, who's one of us, who loves her and she loves him. . . .

(*Helen rushes upstairs.*)

DURAND. Now you've gone too far, Theresa.

MRS. DURAND. I know what's best. I know her better than she does herself. I don't want her to be another Belle. . . . Father, I think it time Helen married.

DURAND (*slowly*). So do I.

MRS. DURAND. I'll talk to Mrs. Carrington tomorrow. We'll make the arrangements for next month.

> *Dissolve to the office of the engineer for the housing project: a plain prefabricated room with a desk, blueprints and so forth. Welch and an assistant are at work on a set of plans.*

ASSISTANT. Oh, say, Ned, what about the old shed?

NED. We'll tear it down Friday. Unless they call out the Marines to stop us.

ASSISTANT. That old woman is certainly persistent. The

president of the Bird Refuge Society was here this morning, saying birds roosted in the shed and . . .

(A knock on the door. Assistant opens it. Belle enters, very shy.)

BELLE. Could I see Mr. Welch, please?

NED. Come in.

BELLE. I'm Mrs. Travers, Helen's aunt. We live in the house over there, across the way.

NED. I know. Sit down, please.

ASSISTANT. I'll be right back. Excuse me, Mrs. Travers. *(He goes.)*

NED. I haven't heard a word from your house for two weeks.

BELLE. I can't stay long, but . . . well, I'm not really as bold as I must seem. *(With sudden courage.)* Tell me, you . . . you like Helen, don't you?

NED. Yes, very much. But she won't see me. She won't come to the telephone and she didn't answer a letter I sent. So I gave up. Anyway, we're nearly finished down here and I'll be going home soon.

BELLE. Before you go, I wish you would see Helen. Oh, I know I'm interfering and Theresa would kill me if she knew, but you see, I want Helen to be happy and, well, she's marrying *him*.

NED. You mean Carrington?

BELLE *(nods)*. On the fourteenth of this month they will be married. The honeymoon will be spent in Charleston, looking at azaleas and visiting relatives. It should have been idyllic, but it isn't.

NED. All she has to do is say "No, I won't marry him." And

106

if she wants to see me, all she has to do is cross a few yards of construction and here I am.

BELLE. She won't because of her mother, because of the family.

NED. You can't tell me that in the middle of the twentieth century there is such a thing as a girl marrying against her will.

BELLE. No, it is not against her will; in fact, it is her will which is forcing to marry against her heart.

NED. Well, what am I to do? I can't ride up to the house on a white horse and kidnap her on her wedding day.

BELLE. Her wedding day might be a little late. But I like the idea of the white horse.

NED. Look, if she's so eager to see me, why hasn't she tried?

BELLE. She gave her word to her mother that she would make no move to see you, and Helen won't break her word. My sister-in-law — Helen's mother — is not really a bad woman, but she is desperate to keep things the way they were. . . .

NED. I know. Every day I get a message from somebody about that old shed out there. . . .

BELLE. That's it exactly. The gazebo . . . the summer pavilion . . . she wants to keep it the way it was, but that's like always keeping summer, isn't it? when there are three other seasons . . . Oh, I've talked such a lot. Excuse me.

NED. I'm glad you did. But in two weeks Helen will be married and I'll be going back to Chicago.

BELLE. To Chicago!

NED. That's where I'm from. You ever been there?

BELLE. Yes, for a short time . . . some years ago. It was in the winter. It was very cold and the wind, oh, how the wind blew off the lake! You never came in contact with a Lester Travers, did you? He was known as . . . as "Bull" Travers. He was a figure in the sports world, a pugilist.

NED. No, I don't think I know him. It's a big city.

BELLE. And that was all twenty years ago! Forgive me for wasting your time like this, but I wanted to . . . to get an impression of you before I gave you the message.

NED. The message?

BELLE. Helen will meet you at Ronsard's tonight, at ten o'clock.

> *Dissolve to Ronsard's that night. Ned and Helen enter by different doors at almost the same time. When they see each other, Ned is delighted and Helen startled.*

HELEN. What . . . what are you doing here?

NED. Meeting you.

HELEN. But I'm supposed to see Winter here.

NED. Not Winter, me.

HELEN. I don't understand. This letter. *(Takes it out.)* Winter says to meet him at Ronsard's at midnight . . . very important. I thought this was a funny place for him. . . .

NED. Your aunt told me you wanted to see me . . . here.

HELEN. Belle! It was Belle who wrote the letter and signed it with Winter's name.

NED. Shall I go?

HELEN. Of course not.

NED. Then let's sit down.

(They go to a table. Waiter comes over.)

NED. Two Pernods.

(A pause.)

HELEN. My mother says Pernod has wormwood in it like absinthe and you'll go mad. But I guess I told you that, didn't I? The other time.

NED. I wrote you a letter.

HELEN. I never got it.

NED. Are you sure?

HELEN. Of course . . . but I'm not surprised. My mother must've taken it.

NED. I used to go down by that old shed . . .

HELEN. By the gazebo, yes, I saw you there once. . . .

NED. And I'd study your house, wondering if I'd see you, wondering what you were doing.

HELEN. How fast the new building has gone up!

NED. Do you like it?

HELEN. Yes, I think I do, but I miss the trees.

NED. We'll plant new ones. You're marrying Winter, aren't you?

HELEN. In two weeks.

NED. I like New Orleans, I've decided. I guess I've got used to it. I like the sense of things being old and going on and on the way they always have, without change.

HELEN *(suddenly intense)*. And I wish sometimes that everything that wasn't brand-new and shiny this morning would disappear in a cloud of smoke!

NED. You don't sound like a Durand.

HELEN. It's only sound and fury. I *am* a Durand. And it's too late to do anything about it.

Cut to the hall of the Durand house. Mrs. Durand is on the telephone.

MRS. DURAND. I tell you that boy of yours, Winter, has been an angel, helping around the house, licking envelopes, though we finally got one of those sponges filled with water where you just run the edge of the envelope over the sponge. It's eminently practical and we don't want our bridegroom getting sick from too much mucilage. *(Laughs gaily.)* That would be the end, wouldn't it? Now, honey, would you put Helen on the line? What? She isn't there? Helen isn't at your house? Oh . . . well, that's funny. I thought she said she was going there. I must've misunderstood her. No, no, I'll see you soon, honey. Yes, yes . . . good-by. *(She hangs up, alarmed.)*

Dissolve to Ronsard's. It is dawn. Ned's arm is around Helen's shoulders.

HELEN *(sleepily)*. It must be late.
NED. Early.
HELEN. What's that light over there, in the window?
NED. Street lamp.
HELEN. No, it . . . *(Sits up abruptly.)* It's the morning. Ned, we've been here all night.
NED. Let's send out for breakfast.
HELEN. Oh, the family! I've got to go home.
NED. They think you're with Winter. It's all right.

110

HELEN. It's *not* all right. Take me home, Ned.

NED. Yes . . . darling.

(He kisses her and she does not resist.)

HELEN. Ned, my darling . . .

> *Dissolve to the Durand drawing room. Mrs. Durand is asleep in an armchair. Daylight streams in through the window. Mrs. Durand sits up, suddenly awake. She looks at the clock with horror. She goes to the telephone.*

MRS. DURAND. Operator, give me the police. . . . Hello? This is Theresa Carter Durand of Audubon Park . . .

> *Cut to hall as the front door opens and Ned and Helen enter. Mrs. Durand turns.*

MRS. DURAND. I'm sorry, officer, she's here now. Thank you. *(She hangs up.)*

HELEN. Mother, I am sorry. You shouldn't have waited up.

MRS. DURAND. *This* is the man you were with all night?

HELEN. Yes, it's Ned . . . you remember him, don't you?

MRS. DURAND *(to Ned)*. How can you set foot in this house after what you've done? How can you be so cruel?

NED. Cruel? I haven't done anything. We were at Ronsard's and we forgot about the time, that's all.

MRS. DURAND. All! You have destroyed a family . . . are you happy? Does it please you to know that you've come down here and torn up our land and broken my heart?

HELEN. Mother, stop it, please!

MRS. DURAND *(to Helen)*. And you . . . ! A girl two weeks

111

from her marriage day out all night with . . . with this man! Have you no pride, no decency?

HELEN. Mother, it's perfectly innocent . . .

MRS. DURAND. Is this the return for our love? Is that crazy Durand blood coming out in you the way it did in Belle?

(Belle and Father Durand descend the stairs, in their night clothes.)

MRS. DURAND. Are you going to follow this man to Chicago the way she did? Are you? Is history to repeat itself despite my warning?

(Belle crosses to Helen, embraces her, a little frightened.)

BELLE. Helen . . . dear.

HELEN. It's all right, Aunt Belle!

MRS. DURAND. There they are! Look at them, Father Durand . . . feast your eyes on your daughter and granddaughter! Are you pleased with them, with the pirate blood, are you proud? I'm only a mother. I have no pride left in me . . . only shame!

DURAND. Be careful, Theresa, what you say.

MRS. DURAND. I am the only one *ever* to exert caution! Well, I shall be cautious. I shall do the right thing. Helen, you have made your choice and I am through with you. I shall inform the Carringtons the wedding is off. One of us must show some decency and I'll be the one. . . .

(She starts up the stairs.)

BELLE. Now, Theresa, it's not that serious.

MRS. DURAND. Not to you. Of course it's not serious to you. We know *your* weakness. We have lived with *your* mistake, with *your* shame hanging over us . . .

NED. Look, Mrs. Durand, I think you ought to know . . .

MRS. DURAND. That this family is ruined, yes, I think I ought to know that.

DURAND. My dear Theresa . . .

MRS. DURAND. I could not be the man of the family. It was too much, I realize now. Perhaps it was a mistake to try.

DURAND *(sternly)*. That will be enough, Theresa. This is my house. Helen is my granddaughter no matter what she does.

BELLE. Yes, this is our house. She is our blood.

(Mrs. Durand stops on the stairs.)

MRS. DURAND. So there is to be a league against me in the house I have held together for thirty years. This is my reward. My daughter ruined . . .

HELEN. Mother, I am not ruined. If you would only listen for just one second you would know that Ned and I are going to be married!

MRS. DURAND *(stunned)*. Married! Oh, no, no, this can't be happening to me!

HELEN. It isn't happening to you, Mother . . . it's happening to me!

> *Mrs. Durand turns away, aghast, as we fade out.*

Act Three

*Fade in on the drawing room. It is late aft-
ernoon, a week later. Belle is arranging a tea
service: the teapot's handle is broken, the
cups are chipped. Durand enters.*

DURAND. The best silver?

BELLE. The best. Theresa asked me to arrange a high tea.
I can't think why.

DURAND. Well, I am immediately suspicious. She has been
wandering about the house for a week like Medea on
the eve of murder.

BELLE. This morning she said, "Belle, honey, you get the
silver polished and we're going to have a tea party."

DURAND. Perhaps she's trapped the governor into coming
here, to talk about the gazebo. Where's Helen?

BELLE. She just got in from the school. She's upstairs, getting ready for tea.

DURAND. I like her young man.

BELLE. So do I, but I wish Theresa would be more reasonable. She's refused to see him all week.

DURAND. Poor Theresa, so passionate, so impossible. . . .

BELLE. Helen told me they had no idea of being married
on such short notice until Theresa made her scene and

now they really are in love. *(Sighs.)* In love . . . what
a long time it's been since I've said that phrase!

DURAND. We are well out of all that, aren't we?

BELLE. Yes, we are well out of it.

(Helen enters.)

HELEN. What is Mother up to?

DURAND. No one knows. A mysterious tea party. A sullen
hostess. I anticipate disaster.

HELEN. Mother spoke to me for the first time this morning,
for the first time since the trouble. . . .

BELLE. I'm sure she regrets the line she took.

HELEN. I hope so.

DURAND. How is Ned?

HELEN. Nearly finished with the project. *(Goes to the window.)* It does look wonderful, doesn't it? So new . . .
so tall.

BELLE. Have you thought where you and Ned are going to
live, honey?

HELEN. Chicago. We're going to Chicago right after the
wedding. I can't wait!

BELLE. Chicago!

(Mrs. Durand enters, exuberant.)

MRS. DURAND. That looks very nice, Belle, very nice, but
the cups, oh, my lovely cups are so worn and chipped
. . . we must be careful not to cut our lips. What a becoming color, Helen! I always love you in blue . . . it
was never *my* color, but then my complexion is more
fair than yours. *(Looks about.)* I see our guest has not
yet arrived.

DURAND. Who *is* our distinguished guest?

MRS. DURAND. That is my little secret. Belle honey, get the hot water now.

(Belle goes.)

DURAND. I am too old to enjoy mysteries.

MRS. DURAND *(gaily)*. But I love to mystify, Father Durand. Don't deprive me of my innocent pleasures.

(Doorbell rings. Mrs. Durand goes to answer it, returns with Ned.)

MRS. DURAND. And here he is, my mystery guest!

HELEN. Ned!

NED. Hi, Helen. Mrs. Durand . . . sir.

(He pauses awkwardly as Mrs. Durand swoops down on him and leads him to a sofa where she plumps him beside herself.)

MRS. DURAND. As you see, I have bowed to the inevitable and I have invited my son-in-law-to-be to his future home.

HELEN. Future home?

NED *(pleased)*. Your mother and I had a long session yesterday . . .

MRS. DURAND. Indeed we did! I wended my way through that no man's land between here and the project and we had the nicest chat, deep in enemy country. . . .

HELEN *(to Ned)*. I thought we were going to Chicago.

NED. For a trip. . . .

MRS. DURAND. On your honeymoon, and then back to New Orleans, where he can find work any day of the week and be a credit to us all. Isn't that right, Ned?

NED. Well, I'm not so sure about being a credit . . . oh, hello, Miss Durand.

(Belle has entered.)

BELLE. I thought it was your voice, Mr. Welch.

MRS. DURAND *(while pouring tea)*. On my own honeymoon we went to Europe. I thought that was a trifle far afield, but I have no serious prejudice against foreign climes, and travel does broaden the mind. We went as far east as the country of Egypt, an extremely dirty place — sugar? — in those days but filled with memorable sights — one lump or two? That metal camel you see over there came from Cairo, where they have so many flies and the Sphinx. This is your tea.

NED. I don't think Illinois will be quite as interesting.

HELEN. Oh, I do!

MRS. DURAND. Of course it will be! *(To Helen.)* Mr. Welch and I have such a lot in common. You'd be surprised.

HELEN *(softly)*. I am, Mother, I am.

MRS. DURAND. I judged him out of hand, I fear, on principle, and that is always wrong.

> *Mrs. Durand, Belle and Ned form one group around the tea things. Mrs. Durand pours as she talks. Durand is farther off, outside the immediate circle of Mrs. Durand's conversation. Helen, bewildered, goes to sit beside her grandfather. They talk softly. Cut to them. Mrs. Durand is now merely a murmur in the background.*

HELEN. What is she up to?

DURAND. She is winning him over.

HELEN. I thought she hated him.

DURAND. Of course she does, but since she can't stop the marriage she means to direct it.

HELEN. Did you hear Ned? He's talking about living down here, not going North as we planned.

DURAND. Your mother is cunning.

HELEN. But what on earth can I do?

DURAND. You are her daughter.

HELEN *(nods)*. And I'm helpless.

DURAND. No, you're not helpless. That's what I mean when I say you are her daughter. You can be as strong as she. You're very like her in many ways, so fight her. It's worth it! You don't dare let her win him, do you?

HELEN. No, no, I don't . . . and I won't.

DURAND. Then shall we "unleash the dogs of war"?

HELEN *(suddenly hard)*. Yes . . . yes, I think I shall.

Cut to Mrs. Durand's group. Mrs. Durand is now laughing gaily.

MRS. DURAND. What a delicious sense of humor you have, Ned! My goodness, what a ridiculous wit. . . . Helen honey, you're not laughing? Didn't you hear the story, baby?

HELEN. Yes. It's very funny.

MRS. DURAND. Ned has such a fund of humorous stories. Just like your father, Heaven rest his soul.
(Helen crosses to Mrs. Durand, sits down. Durand gestures to Ned.)

DURAND. Come sit over here, Ned.

MRS. DURAND. No fair, Father Durand, stealing the guest of honor all for yourself.

DURAND. But I shall have such a short time on earth with him, while you, Theresa, will have him for another thirty years from the looks of those cast-iron arteries of yours!

MRS. DURAND. Father Durand! *(To Ned.)* Go humor him before he insults us all mortally and to the quick! *(Ned crosses to Durand.)*

DURAND *(low voice)*. I see she's hooked you.

NED. She's not half as bad as I thought.

DURAND. She is out to charm you.

NED. Well, that's a lot better than being denounced as a savage every five minutes. And down here it's important to get along with your in-laws. *(Gestures.)* You know, this house, this park, sort of gets under your skin. I'm beginning to like it.

DURAND. Even though you are looking straight at me — a bad example?

NED. Oh, you've had a perfect life, doing what you wanted, reading and thinking and . . . and everything.

DURAND. I have been happy, yes. But it was not a perfect life. You see, nothing was done. Though I concede that the perfect shape is a circle. And in a way my life has re-created the perfect shape: my life has been a zero.

> *Cut to the door as Winter Carrington enters, carrying a potted begonia. He is startled by the gathering.*

WINTER. Oh, I'm sorry, Miss Theresa. I didn't know there was a family conclave going on.

MRS. DURAND *(rises)*. Winter, come in! Come in! Now we are all together, one big happy family. What's that thing you're carrying, honey?

WINTER. It's one of Mother's prize begonias. She wanted you to have it. I hope it's all right, my coming here . . .

MRS. DURAND. Of course! Besides, I want you and Ned to know each other, to be good friends. Put that thing over there, will you?

NED. No hard feelings, Winter.

(They shake hands solemnly.)

WINTER. No hard feelings. As Mother would say, it doesn't matter whether you win or lose but how you play the game. I congratulate you.

NED. That's very nice of you, Winter.

MRS. DURAND. Now you must have some tea, Winter, and tell us how that angel incarnate your mother is.

(Winter sits beside her on the sofa.)

WINTER. Mother's been kind of poorly lately. Doctor thinks it's hepatitis.

MRS. DURAND. No, *not* hepatitis! I'm so sorry. Everybody seems to be getting it these days. I read somewhere it comes from the spray they put on apples.

WINTER. Mother doesn't like apples.

MRS. DURAND. Well, it's probably in the air. Helen, it's Winter. Say hello, honey.

HELEN. Hello, Winter. Welcome to the family.

MRS. DURAND. Ignore Miss Sly-puss! Oh, and before I forget, we have great news in this house.

WINTER. You mean the wedding?

MRS. DURAND. I should say second-great news: the wedding of course is next week, but something almost as good . . . you tell them, Ned.

NED. Well, it's about the . . . the shed — I mean, the pavilion in the yard — we've decided — I've decided — to leave it the way it is. I gave the order this morning.

HELEN. It's *not* being torn down?

NED. No, your mother and I talked it over yesterday . . .

HELEN. But it spoils the whole look of the project.

MRS. DURAND. Helen baby, which side are you on?

NED. Anyway, it's not that important, so we're leaving it.

MRS. DURAND. Isn't it grand? He's not really a vandal, as I feared . . . he's going to help us keep things lovely, the way they were. Aren't you thrilled, Helen . . . Father? He's one of us now! Like I always say, Heaven helps those who help themselves!

Dissolve from Helen's shocked face to the construction shed. Ned's assistant is on the telephone. He holds memo in hand.

ASSISTANT. North Star Building in Chicago . . . that's right. Oh, hi, George. Got your girl there? Okay, put her on the line, too. I've got a memo from Welch. Yes, that's right, he's getting married . . . real high-class Southern family. You ready? All right, here goes: "I have decided after considerable deliberation" — ha! — "to retain the small building at the entrance to the housing project which belonged formerly to the Durand family and is known as a 'gazebo.'" G-a-z-e-b-o, isn't that a word for you? "The building will need some minor repairs, but it will be a fine memorial to more gracious days . . ." So help me, I'm not making this up! That's what it says, "more gracious days.". . . Sure, he's out of his mind. Yeah. And another Yankee bites the Southern dust!

> *Dissolve to hallway the afternoon of the wedding day. We see guests milling: for the most part, elderly people in ancient finery. Flowers are everywhere. As camera moves through the crowd to the drawing room we hear snatches of talk: "A lovely bride." "Simply radiant." "He is from the North." "A perfect day." "Theresa is so brave." The first familiar face we see is Winter Carrington, talking to Mr. Durand.*

WINTER. The ceremony was very moving, sir, very moving.

DURAND. Do you realize that no one has yet said to me, "You have not lost a granddaughter but gained a grandson"?

WINTER. I don't believe that is the usual thing to say to grandparents, only to parents.

DURAND. I bow, Winter, to your vast knowledge of the usual.

WINTER. Thank you, sir.

(Belle comes up to them, excited and gay.)

BELLE. Isn't it wonderful, Father, a wedding in the house again!

DURAND. Yes, it is.

BELLE. Theresa was the last bride in this house.

(Mrs. Durand, regal and glowing, appears.)

MRS. DURAND. What a day! The whole Garden District is here!

BELLE. I was saying, Theresa, you were the last bride in this house, so many years ago!

MRS. DURAND. Do you remember what the papers said of my appearance: "moonlight on a camellia"? But this is my daughter's day. *(Ned appears.)* And here is my handsome son-in-law!

NED. I feel like I've met a thousand people!

MRS. DURAND. You're just seeing us as we are, that's all, as we really are. But where is Helen? Where is our radiant bride?

NED. I don't know. She was . . .

DURAND. She'll be right back. She had something to do.

MRS. DURAND. Something to do? A bride on her wedding day? You must take her in hand, Ned. Wear the trousers in your family from the very start. My husband did and I never regretted it. Women like to feel a firm hand at the tiller. *(Glances at window.)* Look at that lovely western light! The sun must have changed its position, because lately we haven't had the sunsets, your project being in the way. My, I've never seen such a sunset, such a heavenly light!

WINTER. Miss Theresa, there's a fire down there in the yard!

(All rush to terrace, except Durand and Belle.)

MRS. DURAND. Oh, no . . . not the pavilion! *(Turns.)* Who did this? Who set fire to it? *(To Ned.)* It was you . . . you told them to burn it! You vandal . . . you devil! You set that fire!

NED *(stammers)*. I didn't. I don't know how it started.

123

(Helen has entered in her bridal veil.)

HELEN. I set the fire, Mother.

MRS. DURAND. You?

HELEN. It was my present to Ned, my wedding gift.

MRS. DURAND. You're insane!

(She sits down heavily on a bench, the firelight in her face. Guests murmur in the background.)

HELEN. The pavilion spoiled everything. He only left it because of us. I couldn't let him do that.

MRS. DURAND *(softly)*. I used to sit there on summer nights . . .

HELEN. Mother, it's gone. Give it up. *(She crosses to Ned, who takes her arm.)* We're going to Chicago, aren't we?

NED. I guess we'll have to. I mean, sure . . . sure, we'll go, Helen. If that's what you want.

HELEN. That's what I want.

DURAND *(dryly)*. Just like your mother. The line of succession goes on.

HELEN *(in her mother's voice)*. Heaven helps those who help themselves!

(Belle hugs both bride and groom.)

BELLE. Oh, it's all so wonderful, like a fairy tale! The spell is broken.

(Durand crosses to Theresa. He comforts her.)

DURAND. Don't weep, Daughter. Life isn't over because an old shed was burned down on a wedding day.

MRS. DURAND *(weeping)*. They have taken everything now . . . everything is gone. And I tried so hard, so very hard . . .

(She rises and goes inside, leaving the others on the

terrace. Mrs. Carrington, a great frump of a woman, bears down on Ned and Helen.)

MRS. CARRINGTON. Mr. Welch, I am the mother of Winter Carrington and I feel I know you already. *(Sees fire.)* Oh, why, look at that bonfire out there! Isn't that something? Trust Theresa to do the right thing. In olden times we always had bonfires on special occasions, bonfires and fireworks. . . . My, what a gorgeous sight! And if I know my Theresa there'll be fireworks at dusk. *(Sighs.)* Oh, what a lovely wedding it was, Helen, little Helen . . . and how like your sainted mother you look in that glorious lace, just like your mother all over again.

Cut to Mrs. Durand, grim, on the stairs.
Cut back to terrace.

MRS. CARRINGTON. How I wept when I saw you in the church and thought of Theresa's wedding, and everything happening all over again, and now tonight, tonight fireworks on the lawn . . . !

Fade out on Helen, her mother reborn.

Yes, my debts to Tennessee Williams and Anton Chekhov are suspiciously large, but I say in my defense that the loans were made honorably and with open eyes: I appropriated the theme of *The Cherry Orchard* so that I might twist it about and make a new point. I wanted to show how so very often one generation, in freeing itself of its predecessor, becomes that predecessor. In *Summer Pavilion* the daughter can only defeat her mother by becoming her mother; at the play's end it should be evident that the girl, victorious now, will one day herself be imperiled by time and change and the will of others, her own gazebo swept away. . . . Life is a chain and none of us differs too much from what went before.

To me the chief pleasure of this production was working with Miriam Hopkins, an actress in the great tradition, blazing with energy and light. Watching her build a performance is a unique experience: she is ruthless in her determination to create something splendid and the result, at least in this case, was certainly worth the effort.

Visit to a Small Planet

Performed May 8, 1955
on
The Goodyear Television Playhouse (NBC)

Produced by Gordon Duff
Associate Producer: Robert Alan Aurther
Directed by Jack Smight

The Cast

KRETON	Cyril Ritchard
ROGER SPELDING	Edward Andrews
ELLEN SPELDING	Jill Kraft
MRS. SPELDING	Sylvia Davis
JOHN RANDOLPH	Dick York
GENERAL POWERS	Alan Reed
AIDE	Bruce Kirby
PAUL LAURENT	Theodore Bikel
SECOND VISITOR	Louis Edmonds
PRESIDENT OF PARAGUAY	Alfred de la Fuente

Act One

Stock shot: The night sky, stars. Then slowly a luminous object arcs into view. As it is almost upon us, dissolve to the living room of the Spelding house in Maryland.

Superimpose card: THE TIME: THE DAY AFTER TOMORROW.

The room is comfortably balanced between the expensively decorated and the homely. Roger Spelding is concluding his TV broadcast. He is middle-aged, unctuous, resonant. His wife, bored and vague, knits passively while he talks at his desk. Two technicians are on hand, operating the equipment.

His daughter Ellen, a lively girl of twenty, fidgets as she listens.

SPELDING (*into microphone*). . . . and so, according to General Powers — who should know if anyone does — the flying object which has given rise to so much irresponsible conjecture is nothing more than a meteor passing through the earth's orbit. It is not, as many believe, a secret weapon of this country. Nor is it a spaceship, as certain lunatic elements have suggested. General Powers has assured me that it is highly doubtful there is any form of life on other planets capable of building a spaceship. "If any traveling is to be done in space, we will do it first." And those are his exact words. . . . Which winds up another week of news. (*Crosses to pose with wife and daughter.*) This is Roger Spelding, saying good night to Mother and Father America from my old homestead in Silver Glen, Maryland, close to the warm pulse beat of the nation.

TECHNICIAN. Good show tonight, Mr. Spelding.

SPELDING. Thank you.

TECHNICIAN. Yes, sir, you were right on time.

(*Technicians switch off microphone. Spelding rises wearily, his mechanical smile and heartiness suddenly gone.*)

MRS. SPELDING. Very nice, dear. Very nice.

TECHNICIAN. See you next week, Mr. Spelding.

SPELDING. Thank you, boys.

(*Technicians go.*)

SPELDING. Did you like the broadcast, Ellen?

ELLEN. Of course I did, Daddy.

SPELDING. Then what did I say?

ELLEN. Oh, that's not fair.

SPELDING. It's not very flattering when one's own daughter won't listen to what one says while millions of people . . .

ELLEN. I always listen, Daddy, you know that.

MRS. SPELDING. We love your broadcasts, dear. I don't know what we'd do without them.

SPELDING. Starve, I suspect.

ELLEN. I wonder what's keeping John?

SPELDING. Certainly not work.

ELLEN. Oh, Daddy, stop it! John works very hard and you know it.

MRS. SPELDING. Yes, he's a perfectly nice boy, Roger. I like him.

SPELDING. I know, I know. He has every virtue except the most important one: he has no get-up-and-go.

ELLEN *(precisely)*. He doesn't want to get up and he doesn't want to go because he's already where he wants to be, on his own farm, which is exactly where *I'm* going to be when we're married.

SPELDING. More thankless than a serpent's tooth is an ungrateful child.

ELLEN. I don't think that's right. Isn't it "more deadly . . ."?

SPELDING. Whatever the exact quotation is, I stand by the sentiment.

MRS. SPELDING. Please, don't quarrel. It always gives me a headache.

SPELDING. I never quarrel. I merely reason, in my simple way, with Miss Know-it-all here.

ELLEN. Oh, Daddy! Next you'll tell me I should marry for money.

SPELDING. There is nothing wrong with marrying a wealthy man. The horror of it has always eluded me. However, my only wish is that you marry someone hard-working, ambitious, a man who'll make his mark in the world. Not a boy who plans to sit on a farm all his life, growing peanuts.

ELLEN. English walnuts.

SPELDING. Will you stop correcting me?

ELLEN. But, Daddy, John grows walnuts . . .

(John enters, breathlessly.)

JOHN. Come out! Quick! It's coming this way! It's going to land right here!

SPELDING. *What's* going to land?

JOHN. The spaceship. Look!

SPELDING. Apparently you didn't hear my broadcast. The flying object in question is a meteor, not a spaceship.

(John has gone out with Ellen. Spelding and Mrs. Spelding follow.)

MRS. SPELDING. Oh, my! Look! Something *is* falling! Roger, you don't think it's going to hit the house, do you?

SPELDING. The odds against being hit by a falling object that size are, I should say, roughly, ten million to one.

JOHN. Ten million to one or not, it's going to land right here and it's *not* falling.

SPELDING. I'm sure it's a meteor.

MRS. SPELDING. Shouldn't we go down to the cellar?

SPELDING. If it's not a meteor, it's an optical illusion . . . mass hysteria.

ELLEN. Daddy, it's a real spaceship. I'm sure it is.

SPELDING. Or maybe a weather balloon. Yes, that's what it is. General Powers said only yesterday . . .

JOHN. It's landing!

SPELDING. I'm going to call the police . . . the army! *(Bolts inside.)*

ELLEN. Here it comes . . . oh, look how it shines!

JOHN. How soft it lands!

132

MRS. SPELDING. Right in my rose garden!

ELLEN. Maybe it's a balloon.

JOHN. No, it's a spaceship and right there in your own back yard.

ELLEN. What makes it shine so?

JOHN. I don't know, but I'm going to find out. *(Runs off toward the light.)*

ELLEN. Oh, darling, don't! Darling, please. John, John come back!

(Spelding, wide-eyed, returns.)

MRS. SPELDING. Roger, it's landed right in my rose garden.

SPELDING. I got General Powers. He's coming over. He said they've been watching this thing. They . . . they don't know what it is.

ELLEN. You mean it's nothing of ours?

SPELDING. They believe it . . . *(Swallows hard.)* . . . it's from outer space.

ELLEN. And John's down there! Daddy, get a gun or something.

SPELDING. Perhaps we'd better leave the house until the Army gets here.

ELLEN. We can't leave John.

SPELDING. I can. *(Peers nearsightedly.)* Why, it's not much larger than a car. I'm sure it's some kind of meteor.

ELLEN. Meteors are blazing hot.

SPELDING. This is a cold one.

ELLEN. It's opening . . . the whole side's opening! *(Shouts.)* John! Come back! Quick!

MRS. SPELDING. Why, there's a man getting out of it! *(Sighs.)* I feel much better already. I'm sure if we ask

133

him, he'll move that thing for us. Roger, you ask him.

SPELDING *(ominously)*. If it's really a man?

ELLEN. John's shaking hands with him. *(Calls.)* John darling, come on up here . . .

MRS. SPELDING. And bring your friend.

SPELDING. There's something wrong with the way that creature looks . . . if it is a man and not a . . . not a monster.

MRS. SPELDING. He looks perfectly nice to me.

(John and the visitor appear. The visitor is in his forties, a mild, pleasant-looking man with side whiskers and dressed in the fashion of 1860. When he sees the three people, he pauses in silence for a moment. They stare back at him, equally interested.)

VISITOR. I seem to've made a mistake. I *am* sorry. I'd better go back and start over again.

SPELDING. My dear sir, you've only just arrived. Come in, come in. I don't need to tell you what a pleasure this is . . . Mister . . . Mister . . .

VISITOR. Kreton. . . . This *is* the wrong costume, isn't it?

SPELDING. Wrong for what?

KRETON. For the country, and the time.

SPELDING. Well, it's a trifle old-fashioned.

MRS. SPELDING. But really awfully handsome.

KRETON. Thank you.

MRS. SPELDING *(to husband)*. Ask him about moving that thing off my rose bed.

(Spelding leads them all into the living room.)

SPELDING. Come in and sit down. You must be tired after your trip.

KRETON. Yes, I am a little. *(Looks around delightedly.)* Oh, it's better than I'd hoped!

SPELDING. Better? What's better?

KRETON. The house . . . that's what you call it? Or is this an apartment?

SPELDING. This is a house in the state of Maryland, U.S.A.

KRETON. In the late twentieth century! To think this is really the twentieth century. I must sit down a moment and collect myself. The *real* thing! *(He sits down.)*

ELLEN. You . . . you're not an American, are you?

KRETON. What a nice thought! No, I'm not.

JOHN. You sound more English.

KRETON. Do I? Is my accent very bad?

JOHN. No, it's quite good.

SPELDING. Where *are* you from, Mr. Kreton?

KRETON *(evasively)*. Another place.

SPELDING. On this earth of course.

KRETON. No, not on this planet.

ELLEN. Are you from Mars?

KRETON. Oh dear no, not Mars. There's nobody on Mars . . . at least no one I know.

ELLEN. I'm sure you're teasing us and this is all some kind of publicity stunt.

KRETON. No, I really am from another place.

SPELDING. I don't suppose you'd consent to my interviewing you on television?

KRETON. I don't think your authorities will like that. They are terribly upset as it is.

SPELDING. How do you know?

KRETON. Well, I . . . pick up things. For instance, I know

that in a few minutes a number of people from your Army will be here to question me and they — like you — are torn by doubt.

SPELDING. How extraordinary!

ELLEN. Why did you come here?

KRETON. Simply a visit to your small planet. I've been studying it for years. In fact, one might say you people are my hobby. Especially this period of your development.

JOHN. Are you the first person from your . . . your planet to travel in space like this?

KRETON. Oh my no! Everyone travels who wants to. It's just that no one wants to visit you. I can't think why. *I* always have. You'd be surprised what a thorough study I've made. *(Recites.)* The planet Earth is divided into five continents with a number of large islands. It is mostly water. There is one moon. Civilization is only just beginning. . . .

SPELDING. Just beginning! My dear sir, we have had . . .

KRETON *(blandly).* You are only in the initial stages — the most fascinating stages, as far as I'm concerned. . . . I do hope I don't sound patronizing.

ELLEN. Well, we are very proud.

KRETON. I know and that's one of your most endearing, primitive traits. Oh, I can't believe I'm here at last!
(General Powers, a vigorous product of the National Guard, and his aide enter.)

POWERS. All right, folks. The place is surrounded by troops. Where is the monster?

KRETON. I, my dear General, am the monster.

POWERS. What are you dressed up for, a fancy-dress party?

KRETON. I'd hoped to be in the costume of the period. As you see, I am about a hundred years too late.

POWERS. Roger, who is this joker?

SPELDING. This is Mr. Kreton . . . General Powers. Mr. Kreton arrived in that thing outside. He is from another planet.

POWERS. I don't believe it.

ELLEN. It's true. We saw him get out of the flying saucer.

POWERS *(to aide)*. Captain, go down and look at that ship. But be careful. Don't touch anything. And don't let anybody else near it. *(Aide goes.)* So you're from another planet.

KRETON. Yes. My, that's a very smart uniform, but I prefer the ones made of metal, the ones you used to wear. You know: with the feathers on top.

POWERS. That was five hundred years ago.

KRETON. As long ago as that!

POWERS. Are you *sure* you're not from the Earth?

KRETON. Yes.

POWERS. Well, I'm not. You've got some pretty tall explaining to do.

KRETON. I am at your service.

POWERS. All right, which planet?

KRETON. None that you have ever heard of.

POWERS. Where is it?

KRETON. You wouldn't know.

POWERS. This solar system?

KRETON. No.

POWERS. Another system?

KRETON. Yes.

POWERS. Look, I don't want to play twenty questions with you. I just want to know where you're from. The law requires it.

KRETON. It's possible that I *could* explain it to a mathematician, but I'm afraid I couldn't explain it to you, not for another five hundred years, and by then, of course, *you'd* be dead, because you people do die, don't you?

POWERS. What?

KRETON. Poor fragile butterflies, such brief little moments in the sun. . . . You see, *we* don't die.

POWERS. You'll die all right if it turns out you're a spy or a hostile alien.

KRETON. I'm sure you wouldn't be so cruel.

(Aide returns; he looks disturbed.)

POWERS. What did you find?

AIDE. I'm not sure, General.

POWERS *(heavily)*. Then do your best to describe what the object is like.

AIDE. Well, it's elliptical, with a fourteen-foot diameter. And it's made of an unknown metal which shines, and inside there isn't anything.

POWERS. Isn't anything?

AIDE. There's nothing inside the ship: no instruments, no food, nothing.

POWERS *(to Kreton)*. What did you do with your instrument board?

KRETON. With my what? Oh, I don't have one.

POWERS. How does the thing travel?

KRETON. I don't know.

POWERS. You don't know! Now, look, mister, you're in

pretty serious trouble. I suggest you do a bit of cooperating. You claim you traveled here from outer space in a machine with no instruments . . .

KRETON. Well, these cars are rather common in my world and I suppose, once upon a time, I must've known the theory on which they operate, but I've long since forgotten. After all, General, we're not mechanics, you and I.

POWERS. Roger, do you mind if we use your study?

SPELDING. Not at all. Not at all, General.

POWERS. Mr. Kreton and I are going to have a chat. *(To aide.)* Put in a call to the Chief of Staff.

AIDE. Yes, General.

(Spelding rises, leads Kreton and Powers into next room, a handsomely furnished study, many books, globes of the world, and so forth.)

SPELDING. This way, gentlemen.

(Kreton sits down comfortably beside the globe, which he twirls thoughtfully. At the door, Spelding speaks in a low voice to Powers.)

SPELDING. I hope I'll be the one to get the story first, Tom.

POWERS. There isn't any story. Complete censorship. And by the way, this house is under martial law. I've a hunch we're in trouble.

(He shuts the door. Spelding turns and rejoins his family.)

ELLEN. I think he's wonderful, whoever he is.

MRS. SPELDING. I wonder how much damage he did to my rose garden. . . .

JOHN. It's sure hard to believe he's really from outer space.

No instruments, no nothing . . . boy, they must be advanced scientifically.

MRS. SPELDING. Is he spending the night, dear?

SPELDING. What?

MRS. SPELDING. Is he spending the night?

SPELDING. Oh, yes, yes, I suppose he will be.

MRS. SPELDING. Then I'd better go make up the bedroom. He seems perfectly nice to me. I like his whiskers. They're so very . . . comforting. Like Grandfather Spelding's. (*She goes.*)

SPELDING (*bitterly*). I *know* this story will leak out before I can interview him. I just know it.

ELLEN. What does it mean, we're under martial law?

SPELDING. It means we have to do what General Powers tells us to do. (*Goes to window. Soldier passes by.*) See?

JOHN. I wish I'd taken a closer look at that ship when I had the chance.

ELLEN. Perhaps he'll give us a ride in it.

JOHN. Traveling in space! Just like those stories. You know: intergalactic-drive stuff.

SPELDING. *If* he's not an imposter.

ELLEN. I have a feeling he isn't.

JOHN. Well, I better call the family and tell them I'm all right. (*He crosses to telephone by the door which leads into the hall.*)

AIDE. I'm sorry, sir, but you can't use the phone.

SPELDING. He certainly can. This is my house . . .

AIDE (*mechanically*). This house is a military reservation until the crisis is over — order of General Powers. I'm sorry.

JOHN. Just how am I to call home to say where I am?

AIDE. Only General Powers can help you. You're also forbidden to leave this house without permission.

SPELDING. You can't do this!

AIDE. I'm afraid, sir, we've done it.

ELLEN. Isn't it exciting!

Cut to study.

POWERS. Are you deliberately trying to confuse me?

KRETON. Not deliberately, no.

POWERS. We have gone over and over this for two hours now and all that you've told me is that you're from another planet in another solar system . . .

KRETON. In another dimension. I think that's the word you use.

POWERS. In another dimension, and you have come here as a tourist.

KRETON. Up to a point, yes. What did you expect?

POWERS. It is my job to guard the security of this country.

KRETON. I'm sure that must be very interesting work.

POWERS. For all I know, you are a spy, sent here by an alien race to study us, preparatory to invasion.

KRETON. Oh, none of my people would *dream* of invading you.

POWERS. How do I know that's true?

KRETON *(blandly)*. You don't, so I suggest you believe me. I should also warn you: I can tell what's inside.

POWERS. What's inside?

KRETON. What's inside your mind.

POWERS. You're a mind reader?

KRETON. I don't really read it. I hear it.

POWERS. What am I thinking?

KRETON. That I am either a lunatic from the Earth or a spy from another world.

POWERS. Correct. But then you could've guessed that. *(Frowns.)* What am I thinking now?

KRETON. You're making a picture. Three silver stars. You're pinning them on your shoulder, instead of the two stars you now wear.

POWERS *(startled)*. That's right. I was thinking of my promotion.

KRETON. If there's anything I can do to hurry it along, just let me know.

POWERS. You can. Tell me why you're here.

KRETON. Well, we don't travel much, my people. We used to, but since we see everything through special monitors and re-creators, there is no particular need to travel. However, I am a hobbyist. I love to gad about.

POWERS *(taking notes)*. Are you the first to visit us?

KRETON. Oh no! We started visiting you long before there were people on the planet. However, we are seldom noticed on our trips. I'm sorry to say I slipped up, coming in the way I did . . . but then this visit was all rather impromptu. *(Laughs.)* I am a creature of impulse, I fear. *(Aide looks in.)*

AIDE. Chief of Staff on the telephone, General.

POWERS *(picks up phone)*. Hello, yes, sir. Powers speaking. I'm talking to him now. No, sir. No, sir. No, we can't determine what method of power was used. He won't talk. Yes, sir. I'll hold him here. I've put the house under martial law . . . belongs to a friend of mine, Roger Spel-

ding, the TV commentator. Roger Spelding, the TV . . .
What? Oh, no, I'm sure he won't say anything. Who
. . . oh, yes, sir. Yes, I realize the importance of it. Yes,
I will. Good-by. *(Hangs up.)* The President of the United
States wants to know all about you.

KRETON. How nice of him! And I want to know all about
him. But I do wish you'd let me rest a bit first. Your
language is still not familiar to me. I had to learn them
all. Quite exhausting.

POWERS. You speak *all* our languages?

KRETON. Yes, all of them. But then it's easier than you
might think since I can see what's inside.

POWERS. Speaking of what's inside, we're going to take
your ship apart.

KRETON. Oh, I wish you wouldn't.

POWERS. Security demands it.

KRETON. In that case *my* security demands you leave it
alone.

POWERS. You plan to stop us?

KRETON. I already have. *(Beat.)* Listen.

(Far-off shouting. Aide rushes into the study.)

AIDE. Something's happened to the ship, General. The
door's shut and there's some kind of wall all around it,
an invisible wall. We can't get near it.

KRETON *(to camera)*. I hope there was no one inside.

POWERS *(to Kreton)*. How did you do that?

KRETON. I couldn't begin to explain. Now, if you don't
mind, I think we should go in and see our hosts.

*(He rises, goes into the living room. Powers and aide
look at each other.)*

POWERS. Don't let him out of your sight.

*Cut to living room as Powers picks up the
telephone. Kreton is with John and Ellen.*

KRETON. I don't mind curiosity but I really can't permit
them to wreck my poor ship.

ELLEN. What do you plan to do, now you're here?

KRETON. Oh, keep busy. I have a project or two. . . .
(Sighs.) I can't believe you're real!

JOHN. Then we're all in the same boat.

KRETON. Boat? Oh yes! Well, I should've come ages ago
but I . . . I couldn't get away until yesterday.

JOHN. Yesterday? It only took you a *day* to get here?

KRETON. One of *my* days, not yours. But then you don't
know about time yet.

JOHN. Oh, you mean relativity.

KRETON. No, it's much more involved than that. You won't
know about time until . . . now let me see if I remember . . . no, I don't, but it's about two thousand years.

JOHN. What do we do between now and then?

KRETON. You simply go on the way you are, living your exciting primitive lives . . . you have no idea how much
fun you're having now.

ELLEN. I hope you'll stay with us while you're here.

KRETON. That's very nice of you. Perhaps I will. Though
I'm sure you'll get tired of having a visitor under foot
all the time.

ELLEN. Certainly not. And Daddy will be deliriously happy.
He can interview you by the hour.

JOHN. What's it like in outer space?

KRETON. Dull.

ELLEN. I should think it would be divine!

(Powers enters.)

KRETON. No, General, it won't work.

POWERS. What won't work?

KRETON. Trying to blow up my little force field. You'll just plow up Mrs. Spelding's garden.

(Powers snarls.)

ELLEN. Can you tell what we're *all* thinking?

KRETON. Yes. As a matter of fact, it makes me a bit giddy. Your minds are not at all like ours. You see, we control our thoughts, while you . . . well, it's extraordinary the things you think about!

ELLEN. Oh, how awful! You can tell *everything* we think?

KRETON. Everything. It's one of the reasons I'm here, to intoxicate myself with your primitive minds . . . with the wonderful rawness of your emotions! You have no idea how it excites me! You simply seethe with unlikely emotions.

ELLEN. I've never felt so sordid.

JOHN. From now on I'm going to think about agriculture.

SPELDING *(entering)*. You would.

ELLEN. Daddy!

KRETON. No, no. You must go right on thinking about Ellen. Such wonderfully *purple* thoughts!

SPELDING. Now see here, Powers, you're carrying this martial law thing too far.

POWERS. Unfortunately, until I have received word from Washington as to the final disposition of this problem, you must obey my orders: no telephone calls, no communication with the outside.

SPELDING. This is insupportable.

KRETON. Poor Mr. Spelding! If you like, I shall go. That would solve everything, wouldn't it?

POWERS. You're not going anywhere, Mr. Kreton, until I've had my instructions.

KRETON. I sincerely doubt if you could stop me. However, I put it up to Mr. Spelding. Shall I go?

SPELDING. Yes! (*Powers gestures a warning.*) Do stay, I mean: want you to get a good impression of us . . .

KRETON. And of course you still want to be the first journalist to interview me. Fair enough. All right, I'll stay on for a while.

POWERS. Thank you.

KRETON. Don't mention it.

SPELDING. General, may I ask our guest a few questions?

POWERS. Go right ahead, Roger. I hope you'll do better than I did.

SPELDING. Since you can read our minds, you probably already know what our fears are.

KRETON. I do, yes.

SPELDING. We are afraid that you represent a hostile race.

KRETON. And I have assured General Powers that my people are not remotely hostile. Except for me, no one is interested in this planet's present stage.

SPELDING. Does this mean you might be interested in a *later* stage?

KRETON. I'm not permitted to discuss your future. Of course my friends think me perverse to be interested in a primitive society, but there's no accounting for tastes, is there? You are my hobby. I love you. And that's all there is to it.

POWERS. So you're just here to look around . . . sort of going native.

KRETON. What a nice expression! That's it exactly. I am going native.

POWERS (*grimly*). Well, it is my view that you have been sent here by another civilization for the express purpose of reconnoitering prior to invasion.

KRETON. That *would* be your view! The wonderfully primitive assumption that all strangers are hostile. You're almost too good to be true, General.

POWERS. You deny your people intend to make trouble for us?

KRETON. I deny it.

POWERS. Then are they interested in establishing communication with us? Trade? That kind of thing?

KRETON. We have always had communication with you. As for trade, well, we do not trade . . . that is something peculiar only to your social level. (*Quickly.*) Which I'm not criticizing! As you know, I approve of everything you do.

POWERS. I give up.

SPELDING. You have no interest then in . . . well, trying to dominate the earth?

KRETON. Oh, yes! Didn't I tell you?

POWERS. I thought you just finished saying your people weren't interested in us.

KRETON. *They're* not, but *I* am.

POWERS. You!

KRETON. I, yes. You see, I've come here to take charge.

POWERS. Of the United States?

KRETON. No, of the whole world. I'm sure you'll be much happier and it will be great fun for me. You'll get used to it in no time.

POWERS. This is ridiculous. How can one man take over the world?

KRETON *(gaily)*. Wait and see!

POWERS *(to aide)*. Grab him!

(Powers and aide rush Kreton, but within a foot of him they stop, stunned.)

KRETON. Naughty! Naughty! See? You can't touch me. That's part of the game, too. *(Yawns and stretches.)* Now, if you don't mind, I shall go up to my room for a little lie-down.

SPELDING. I'll show you the way.

KRETON. That's all right. I know the way. *(Touches his brow.)* Such savage thoughts! My head is vibrating like a drum. I feel quite giddy, with all of you thinking at once. *(Starts to door, pauses beside Mrs. Spelding.)* No, it's not a dream, dear lady. I shall be here in the morning when you wake up. And now, good night, dear, wicked children.

He goes as we fade out.

Act Two

Fade in on Kreton's bedroom next morn-
ing. He lies fully clothed on the bed with a
cat on his lap.

KRETON. Poor cat! Of course I sympathize with you. Dogs
are distasteful. What? Oh, I can well believe they do:
yes, yes, how disgusting. They don't ever groom their
fur! But you do *constantly,* such a fine coat. No, no, I'm
not just saying that. I really mean it: exquisite texture.
Of course, I wouldn't say it was *nicer* than skin, but
even so . . . What? Oh, no! They *chase* you! Dogs
chase you for no reason at all except pure malice? You
poor creature. Ah, but you *do* fight back! That's right!
Give it to them: slash, bite, scratch! Don't let them get
away with a trick. . . . No! Do dogs really do that?
Well, I'm sure *you* don't. What . . . oh, well, yes, I
completely agree about mice. They *are* delicious! (Ugh!)
Pounce, snap and there is a heavenly dinner. No, I don't
know any mice yet . . . they're not very amusing? But
after all, think how you must terrify them because you
are so bold, so cunning, so beautifully predatory! *(Knock*
at the door.) Come in.

ELLEN *(enters)*. Good morning. I brought you your break-fast.

KRETON. How thoughtful! *(Examines bacon.)* Delicious, but I'm afraid my stomach is not like yours, if you'll pardon me. I don't eat. *(Removes pill from pocket and swallows it.)* This is all I need for the day. *(Indicates cat.)* Unlike this creature, who would eat her own weight every hour, given a chance.

ELLEN. How do you know?

KRETON. We've had a talk.

ELLEN. You can *speak* to the cat?

KRETON. Not speak exactly, but we communicate. I look inside and the cat coöperates. Bright red thoughts, very exciting, though rather on one level.

ELLEN. Does Kitty like us?

KRETON. No, I wouldn't say she did. But then she has very few thoughts not connected with food. Have you, my quadruped criminal? *(He strokes the cat, which jumps to the floor.)*

ELLEN. You know, you've really upset everyone.

KRETON. I supposed that I would.

ELLEN. Can you really take over the world, just like that?

KRETON. Oh, yes.

ELLEN. What do you plan to do when you *have* taken over?

KRETON. Ah, that is my secret.

ELLEN. Well, I think you'll be a very nice President, *if* they let you, of course.

KRETON. What a sweet girl you are! Marry him right away.

ELLEN. Marry John?

KRETON. Yes. I see it in your head *and* in his. He wants you very much.

ELLEN. Well, we plan to get married this summer, if Father doesn't fuss too much.

KRETON. Do it before then. I shall arrange it all if you like.

ELLEN. How?

KRETON. I can convince your father.

ELLEN. That sounds so ominous! I think you'd better leave poor Daddy alone.

KRETON. Whatever you say. (*Sighs.*) Oh, I love it here. When I woke up this morning I had to pinch myself to prove I was really here.

ELLEN. We were all doing a bit of pinching too. Ever since dawn we've had nothing but visitors and phone calls and troops outside in the garden. No one has the faintest idea what to do about you.

KRETON. Well, I don't think they'll be confused much longer.

ELLEN. How do you plan to conquer the world?

KRETON. I confess I'm not sure. I suppose I must make some demonstration of strength, some colorful trick that will frighten everyone . . . though I much prefer taking charge quietly. That's why I've sent for the President.

ELLEN. The President? *Our* President?

KRETON. Yes, he'll be along any minute now.

ELLEN. But the President just doesn't go around visiting people.

KRETON. He'll visit me. (*Chuckles.*) It may come as a surprise to him, but he'll be in this house in a very few minutes. I think we'd better go downstairs now. (*To cat.*) No, I will not give you a mouse. You must get your own. Be self-reliant. Beast!

*Dissolve to the study. Powers is reading
a book entitled* The Atom and You. *Muf-
fled explosions offstage.*

AIDE *(entering)*. Sir, nothing seems to be working. Do we
have the General's permission to try a fission bomb on
the force field?

POWERS. No . . . no. We'd better give it up.

AIDE. The men are beginning to talk.

POWERS *(thundering)*. Well, keep them quiet! *(Contritely.)*
I'm sorry, Captain. I'm on edge. Fortunately, the whole
business will soon be in the hands of the World Council.

AIDE. What will the World Council do?

POWERS. It will be interesting to observe them.

AIDE. You don't think this Kreton can really take over the
world, do you?

POWERS. Of course not. Nobody can.

*Dissolve to the living room. Mrs. Spelding
and Spelding are alone.*

MRS. SPELDING. You still haven't asked Mr. Kreton about
moving that thing, have you?

SPELDING. There are too many important things to ask
him.

MRS. SPELDING. I hate to be a nag, but you know the trouble I have had getting anything to grow in that part of
the garden . . .

JOHN *(enters)*. Good morning.

MRS. SPELDING. Good morning, John.

JOHN. Any sign of your guest?

MRS. SPELDING. Ellen took his breakfast up to him a few minutes ago.

JOHN. They don't seem to be having much luck, do they? *(To Spelding.)* I sure hope you don't mind my staying here like this.

(Spelding glowers.)

MRS. SPELDING. Why, we love having you! I just hope your family aren't too anxious.

JOHN. One of the G.I.'s finally called them, said I was staying here for the week end.

SPELDING. The rest of our lives, if something isn't done soon.

JOHN. Just how long do you think that'll be, Dad?

SPELDING. Who knows?

(Kreton and Ellen enter.)

KRETON. Ah, how wonderful to see you again! Let me catch my breath. . . . Oh, your minds! It's not easy for me, you know: so many crude thoughts blazing away! Yes, Mrs. Spelding, I will move the ship off your roses.

MRS. SPELDING. That's awfully sweet of you.

KRETON. Mr. Spelding, if any interviews are to be granted, you will be the first, I promise you.

SPELDING. That's very considerate, I'm sure.

KRETON. So you can stop thinking *those* particular thoughts. And now where is the President?

SPELDING. The President?

KRETON. Yes, I sent for him. He should be here. *(Goes to terrace window.)* Ah, that must be he.

(A swarthy man in uniform with a sash across his chest is standing, bewildered, on the terrace. Kreton opens the glass doors.)

153

KRETON. Come in, sir! Come in, Your Excellency. Good of you to come on such short notice.

(Man enters.)

MAN *(in Spanish accent)*. Where am I?

KRETON. You *are* the President, aren't you?

MAN. Of course I am the President. What am I doing here? I was dedicating a bridge and I find myself . . .

KRETON *(aware of his mistake)*. Oh, dear! *Where* was the bridge?

MAN. Where do you think, you idiot, in Paraguay!

KRETON *(to others)*. I seem to've made a mistake. Wrong President. *(Gestures and the man disappears.)* Seemed rather upset, didn't he?

JOHN. You can make people come and go just like that?

KRETON. Just like that.

(Powers looks into room from the study.)

POWERS. Good morning, Mr. Kreton. Could I see you for a moment?

KRETON. By all means. *(He crosses to the study.)*

SPELDING. I believe I am going mad.

> *Cut to study. The aide stands at attention*
> *while Powers addresses Kreton.*

POWERS. . . . and so we feel, the government of the United States feels, that this problem is too big for any one country. Therefore, we have turned the whole affair over to Paul Laurent, the Secretary-General of the World Council.

KRETON. Very sensible. I should've thought of that myself.

POWERS. Mr. Laurent is on his way here now. And may I

add, Mr. Kreton, you've made me look singularly ridiculous.

KRETON. I'm awfully sorry. *(Pause.)* No, you can't kill me.

POWERS. You were reading my mind again.

KRETON. I can't really help it, you know. And such *black* thoughts today, but intense, very intense.

POWERS. I regard you as a menace.

KRETON. I know you do and I think it's awfully unkind. I do mean well.

POWERS. Then go back where you came from and leave us alone.

KRETON. No, I'm afraid I can't do that just yet . . .

(Telephone rings; aide answers it.)

AIDE. He's outside? Sure, let him through. *(To Powers.)* The Secretary-General of the World Council is here, sir.

POWERS *(to Kreton)*. I hope you'll listen to *him*.

KRETON. Oh, I shall, of course. I love listening.

(The door opens. Paul Laurent, middle-aged and serene, enters. Powers and his aide stand at attention. Kreton goes forward to shake hands.)

LAURENT. Mr. Kreton?

KRETON. At your service, Mr. Laurent.

LAURENT. I welcome you to this planet in the name of the World Council.

KRETON. Thank you, sir, thank you.

LAURENT. Could you leave us alone for a moment, General?

POWERS. Yes, sir.

(Powers and the aide go. Laurent smiles at Kreton.)

LAURENT. Shall we sit down?

KRETON. Yes, yes, I love sitting down. I'm afraid my manners are not quite suitable yet.

(They sit down.)

LAURENT. I'm sure they are more than suitable. But now, Mr. Kreton, in violation of all the rules of diplomacy, may I come to the point?

KRETON. You may.

LAURENT. Why are you here?

KRETON. Curiosity. Pleasure.

LAURENT. You are a tourist, then, in this time and place?

KRETON *(nods)*. Yes. Very well put.

LAURENT. We have been informed that you have extraordinary powers.

KRETON. By your standards, yes, they must seem extraordinary.

LAURENT. We have also been informed that it is your intention to . . . to take charge of this world.

KRETON. That is correct. . . . What a remarkable mind you have! I have difficulty looking inside it.

LAURENT *(laughs)*. Practice. I've attended so many conferences. . . . May I say that your conquest of our world puts your status of tourist in a rather curious light?

KRETON. Oh, I said nothing about *conquest*.

LAURENT. Then how else do you intend to govern? The people won't allow you to direct their lives without a struggle.

KRETON. But I'm sure they will if I ask them to.

LAURENT. You believe you can do all this without, well, without violence?

KRETON. Of course I can. One or two demonstrations

and I'm sure they'll do as I ask. *(Smiles.)* Watch this. *(Pause. Then shouting. Powers bursts into room.)*

POWERS. *Now* what've you done?

KRETON. Look out the window, Your Excellency.

(Laurent goes to window. A rifle floats by, followed by an alarmed soldier.)

KRETON. Nice, isn't it? I confess I worked out a number of rather melodramatic tricks last night. Incidentally, all the rifles of all the soldiers in all the world are now floating in the air. *(Gestures.)* Now they have them back.

POWERS *(to Laurent)*. You see, sir, I didn't exaggerate in my report.

LAURENT *(awed)*. No, no, you certainly didn't.

KRETON. You were skeptical, weren't you?

LAURENT. Naturally. But now I . . . now I think it's possible.

POWERS. That this . . . gentleman is going to run everything?

LAURENT. Yes, yes I do. And it might be wonderful.

KRETON. You *are* more clever than the others. You begin to see that I mean only good.

LAURENT. Yes, only good. General, do you realize what this means? We can have one government . . .

KRETON. With innumerable bureaus, and intrigue . . .

LAURENT *(excited)*. And the world could be incredibly prosperous, especially if he'd help us with his superior knowledge. . . .

KRETON *(delighted)*. I will, I will. I'll teach you to look into one another's minds. You'll find it devastating but enlightening: all that self-interest, those *lurid* emotions . . .

LAURENT. No more countries. No more wars . . .

KRETON *(startled)*. What? Oh, but I like a lot of countries. Besides, at this stage of your development you're supposed to have lots of countries and lots of wars . . . innumerable wars. . . .

LAURENT. But you can help us change all that.

KRETON. *Change* all that! My dear sir, I am your friend.

LAURENT. What do you mean?

KRETON. Why, your deepest pleasure is violence. How can you deny that? It is the whole point to you, the whole point to my hobby . . . and you are my hobby, all mine.

LAURENT. But our lives are devoted to *controlling* violence, not creating it.

KRETON. Now, don't take me for an utter fool. After all, I can see into your minds. I can feel your emotions as though they were my own and your emotions are incredibly violent. My dear fellow, don't you *know* what you are?

LAURENT. No, what are we?

KRETON. You are savages. I have returned to the dark ages of an insignificant planet simply because I want the glorious excitement of being among you and reveling in your savagery! There is murder in all your hearts and I love it! It intoxicates me!

LAURENT *(slowly)*. You hardly flatter us.

KRETON. I didn't mean to be rude, but you did ask me why I came here and I've told you.

LAURENT. You have no wish, then, to . . . to help us poor savages.

KRETON. I couldn't even if I wanted to. You won't be civilized for at least two thousand years and you won't reach the level of my people for about a million years.

LAURENT *(sadly)*. Then you have come here only to . . . to observe?

KRETON. No, more than that. I mean to regulate your past times. But don't worry: I won't upset things too much. I've decided I don't want to be known to the people. You will go right on with your countries, your squabbles, the way you always have, while I will *secretly* regulate things through you.

LAURENT. The World Council does not govern. We only advise.

KRETON. Well, I shall advise you and you will advise the governments and we shall have a lovely time.

LAURENT. I don't know what to say. You obviously have the power to do as you please.

KRETON. I'm glad you realize that. Poor General Powers is now wondering if a hydrogen bomb might destroy me. It won't, General.

POWERS. Too bad.

KRETON. Now, Your Excellency, I shall stay in this house until you have laid the groundwork for my first project.

LAURENT. And what is that to be?

KRETON. A war! I want one of your really splendid wars, with all the trimmings, all the noise and the fire . . .

LAURENT. A war! You're joking. Why, at this moment we are working as hard as we know how *not* to have a war.

KRETON. But secretly you want one. After all, it's the one thing your little race does well. You'd hardly want me to deprive you of your simple pleasures, now would you?

LAURENT. I think you must be mad.

KRETON. Not mad, simply a philanthropist. Of course I myself shall get a great deal of pleasure out of a war (the vibrations must be incredible) but I'm doing it mostly for you. Now, if you don't mind, I want you to arrange a few incidents, so we can get one started spontaneously.

LAURENT. I refuse.

KRETON. In that event, I shall select someone else to head the World Council. Someone who *will* start a war. I suppose there exist a few people here who might like the idea.

LAURENT. How can you do such a horrible thing to us? Can't you see that we don't want to be savages?

KRETON. But you have no choice. Anyway, you're just pulling my leg! I'm sure you want a war as much as the rest of them do and that's what you're going to get: the biggest war you've ever had!

LAURENT *(stunned)*. Heaven help us!

KRETON *(exuberant)*. Heaven won't. Oh, what fun it will be! I can hardly wait!

> *He strikes the globe of the world a happy*
> *blow as we fade out.*

Act Three

*Fade in on the study, two weeks later.
Kreton is sitting at desk on which a map is
spread out. He has a pair of dividers and
some models of jet aircraft. Occasionally he
pretends to dive-bomb, imitating the sound
of a bomb going off. Powers enters.*

POWERS. You wanted me, sir?

KRETON. Yes, I wanted those figures on radioactive fall-out.

POWERS. They're being made up now, sir. Anything else?

KRETON. Oh, my dear fellow, why do you dislike me so?

POWERS. I am your military aide, sir. I don't have to answer
that question. It is outside the sphere of my duties.

KRETON. Aren't you at least happy about your promotion?

POWERS. Under the circumstances, no, sir.

KRETON. I find your attitude baffling.

POWERS. Is that all, sir?

KRETON. You have never once said what you thought of my
war plans. Not once have I got a single word of encour-
agement from you, a single compliment . . . only black
thoughts.

POWERS. Since you read my mind, sir, you know what I
think.

KRETON. True, but I can't help but feel that deep down inside of you there is just a twinge of professional jeal-
ousy. You don't like the idea of an outsider playing your
game better than you do. Now confess!

POWERS. I am acting as your aide only under duress.

KRETON *(sadly)*. Bitter, bitter . . . and to think I chose
you especially as my aide. Think of all the other gener-
als who would give anything to have your job.

POWERS. Fortunately, they know nothing about my job.

KRETON. Yes, I do think it wise not to advertise my presence, don't you?

POWERS. I can't see that it makes much difference, since
you seem bent on destroying our world.

KRETON. I'm not going to destroy it. A few dozen cities,
that's all, and not very nice cities either. Think of the
fun you'll have building new ones when it's over.

POWERS. How many millions of people do you plan to kill?

KRETON. Well, quite a few, but they love this sort of thing.
You can't convince me they don't. Oh, I know what
Laurent says. But he's a misfit, out of step with his time.
Fortunately, my new World Council is more reasonable.

POWERS. Paralyzed is the word, sir.

KRETON. You think they don't like me either?

POWERS. You *know* they hate you, sir.

KRETON. But love and hate are so confused in your savage
minds and the vibrations of the one are so very like those
of the other that I can't always distinguish. You see, we
neither love nor hate in my world. We simply have hob-
bies. *(He strokes the globe of the world tenderly.)* But
now to work. Tonight's the big night: first, the sneak attack; then, boom! *(Claps hands gleefully.)*

Dissolve to living room, to John and Ellen.

ELLEN. I've never felt so helpless in my life.

JOHN. Here we all stand around doing nothing while he plans to blow up the world.

ELLEN. Suppose we went to the newspapers . . .

JOHN. He controls the press. When Laurent resigned they didn't even print his speech.

(A gloomy pause.)

ELLEN. What are you thinking about?

JOHN. Walnuts.

(They embrace.)

ELLEN. Can't we do anything?

JOHN. No, I guess there's nothing.

ELLEN *(vehemently).* Oh! I could kill him!

(Kreton and Powers enter.)

KRETON. Oh, very good, Ellen, very good! I've never felt you so violent.

ELLEN. You heard what I said to John?

KRETON. Not in words, but you were absolutely bathed in malevolence.

POWERS. I'll get the papers you wanted, sir. *(Exits.)*

KRETON. I don't think he likes me very much, but your father does. Only this morning he offered to handle my public relations and I said I'd let him. Wasn't that nice of him?

JOHN. I think I'll get some fresh air. *(Goes out through the terrace door.)*

KRETON. Oh, dear! *(Sighs.)* He doesn't like me either. Only your father is really entering the spirit of the game. He's a much better sport than you, my dear.

ELLEN (*exploding*). Sport! That's it! You think we're sport. You think we're animals to be played with. Well, we're not. We're people and we don't want to be destroyed.

KRETON (*patiently*). But *I* am not destroying you. You will be destroying one another of your own free will, as you have always done. I am simply a . . . a kibitzer.

ELLEN. No, you are a vampire!

KRETON. A vampire? You mean I drink blood? Ugh!

ELLEN. No, you drink emotions, our emotions. You'll sacrifice us all for the sake of your . . . your vibrations!

KRETON. *Touché.* Yet what harm am I really doing? It's true I'll enjoy the war more than anybody; but it will be *your* destructiveness, after all, not mine.

ELLEN. You could stop it.

KRETON. So could you.

ELLEN. I?

KRETON. Your race. They could stop altogether, but they won't. And I can hardly intervene in their natural development. The most I can do is help out in small, practical ways.

ELLEN. We are not what you think. We're not so . . . so primitive.

KRETON. My dear girl, just take this one household: your mother dislikes your father but she is too tired to do anything about it so she knits and she gardens and she tries not to think about him. Your father, on the other hand, is bored with all of you. Don't look shocked; he doesn't like you any more than you like him. . . .

ELLEN. Don't say that!

KRETON. I am only telling you the truth. Your father wants you to marry opportunistically; therefore, he objects to John, while you, my girl . . .

(With a fierce cry, Ellen grabs a vase to throw.)

ELLEN. You devil!

(Vase breaks in her hand.)

KRETON. You see? That proves my point perfectly. *(Gently.)* Poor savage, I cannot help what you are. *(Briskly.)* Anyway, you will soon be distracted from your personal problems. Tonight is the night. If you're a good girl, I'll let you watch the bombing.

> *Dissolve to study. Eleven forty-five. Powers and the aide gloomily await the war.*

AIDE. General, isn't there anything we can do?

POWERS. It's out of our hands.

(Kreton, dressed as a hussar, with shako, enters.)

KRETON. Everything on schedule?

POWERS. Yes, sir. Planes left for their targets at twenty-two hundred.

KRETON. Good . . . good. I myself shall take off shortly after midnight to observe the attack firsthand.

POWERS. Yes, sir.

(Kreton goes into the living room, where the family is gloomily assembled.)

KRETON. And now, the magic hour approaches! I hope you're all as thrilled as I am.

SPELDING. You still won't tell us who's attacking whom?

KRETON. You'll know in exactly . . . fourteen minutes.

ELLEN *(bitterly)*. Are we going to be killed too?

KRETON. Certainly not! You're quite safe, at least in the early stages of the war.

ELLEN. Thank you.

MRS. SPELDING. I suppose this will mean rationing again.

SPELDING. Will . . . will we see anything from here?

KRETON. No, but there should be a good picture on the monitor in the study. Powers is tuning in right now.

JOHN *(at window)*. Hey look, up there! Coming this way! *(Ellen joins him.)*

ELLEN. What is it?

JOHN. Why . . . it's *another* one! And it's going to land.

KRETON *(surprised)*. I'm sure you're mistaken. No one would dream of coming here. *(He goes to the window.)*

ELLEN. It's landing!

SPELDING. Is it a friend of yours, Mr. Kreton?

KRETON *(slowly)*. No, no, not a friend . . .

(Kreton retreats to the study; on his way, he inadvertently drops a lace handkerchief beside the sofa.)

JOHN. Here he comes.

ELLEN *(suddenly bitter)*. Now we have two of them.

MRS. SPELDING. My poor roses.

(The new visitor enters in a gleam of light from his ship. He is wearing a most futuristic costume. Without a word, he walks past the awed family into the study. Kreton is cowering behind the globe. Powers and the aide stare, bewildered, as the visitor gestures sternly and Kreton reluctantly removes shako and sword. They communicate by odd sounds.)

VISITOR *(to Powers)*. Please leave us alone.

*Cut to living room as Powers and the aide
enter from the study.*

POWERS *(to Ellen).* Who on earth was that?

ELLEN. It's another one, another visitor.

POWERS. Now we're done for.

ELLEN. I'm going in there.

MRS. SPELDING. Ellen, don't you dare!

ELLEN. I'm going to talk to them. *(Starts to door.)*

JOHN. I'll go, too.

ELLEN *(grimly).* No, alone. I know what I want to say.

*Cut to interior of the study, to Kreton and
the other visitor as Ellen enters.*

ELLEN. I want you both to listen to me . . .

VISITOR. You don't need to speak. I know what you will say.

ELLEN. That you have no right here? That you mustn't . . .

VISITOR. I agree. Kreton has no right here. He is well aware
that it is forbidden to interfere with the past.

ELLEN. The past?

VISITOR *(nods).* You are the past, the dark ages; we are from
the future. In fact, we are *your* descendants on another
planet. We visit you from time to time, but we never interfere because it would change *us* if we did. Fortunately, I have arrived in time.

ELLEN. There won't be a war?

VISITOR. There will be no war. And there will be no memory of any of this. When we leave here you will forget
Kreton and me. Time will seem to turn back to the moment before his arrival.

ELLEN *(to Kreton).* Why did you want to hurt us?

KRETON *(heartbroken).* Oh, but I didn't! I only wanted to have . . . well, to have a little fun, to indulge my hobby . . . against the rules, of course.

VISITOR *(to Ellen).* Kreton is a rarity among us. Mentally and morally he is retarded. He is a child and he regards your period as his toy.

KRETON. A child, now really!

VISITOR. He escaped from his nursery and came back in time to you. . . .

KRETON. And *every*thing went wrong, everything! I wanted to visit 1860 — that's my *real* period — but then something happened to the car and I ended up here; not that I don't find you nearly as interesting, but . . .

VISITOR. We must go, Kreton.

KRETON *(to Ellen).* You did like me just a bit, didn't you?

ELLEN. Yes, yes I did, until you let your hobby get out of hand. *(To visitor.)* What is the future like?

VISITOR. Very serene, very different . . .

KRETON. Don't believe him: it is dull, dull, dull beyond belief! One simply floats through eternity: no wars, no excitement . . .

VISITOR. It is forbidden to discuss these matters.

KRETON. I can't see what difference it makes since she's going to forget all about us anyway.

ELLEN. Oh, how I'd love to see the future . . .

VISITOR. It is against . . .

KRETON. Against the rules. How tiresome you are. *(To Ellen.)* But, alas, you can never pay us a call because you aren't born yet! I mean, where we are you are not. Oh, Ellen dear, think kindly of me, until you forget.

ELLEN. I will.

VISITOR. Come. Time has begun to turn back. Time is bending.

(He starts to the door. Kreton turns conspiratorially to Ellen.)

KRETON. Don't be sad, my girl. I shall be back one bright day, but a bright day in 1860. I dote on the Civil War, so exciting . . .

VISITOR. Kreton!

KRETON. Only next time I think it'll be more fun if the South wins! *(He hurries after the visitor.)*

> *Cut to clock as the hands spin backwards.*
> *Dissolve to the living room, exactly the same*
> *as the first scene: Spelding, Mrs. Spelding,*
> *Ellen.*

SPELDING. There is nothing wrong with marrying a wealthy man. The horror of it has always eluded me. However, my only wish is that you marry someone hard-working, ambitious, a man who'll make his mark in the world. Not a boy who plans to sit on a farm all his life, growing peanuts . . .

ELLEN. English walnuts! And he won't just sit there.

SPELDING. Will you stop contradicting me?

ELLEN. But, Daddy, John grows walnuts . . .

(John enters.)

JOHN. Hello, everybody.

MRS. SPELDING. Good evening, John.

ELLEN. What kept you, darling? You missed Daddy's broadcast.

JOHN. I saw it before I left home. Wonderful broadcast, sir.

SPELDING. Thank you, John.

(John crosses to window.)

JOHN. That meteor you were talking about, well, for a while it looked almost like a spaceship or something. You can just barely see it now.

(Ellen joins him at window. They watch, arms about one another.)

SPELDING. Spaceship! Nonsense! Remarkable what some people will believe, want to believe. Besides, as I said in the broadcast, if there's any traveling to be done in space we'll do it first, and we haven't done it yet. . . .

> *He notices Kreton's handkerchief on sofa and picks it up. They all look at it, puzzled. Cut to a stock shot of the starry night, against which two spaceships vanish in the distance, one serene in its course, the other erratic, as we fade out.*

Visit to a Small Planet was the most successful of my television plays. It was written in three days, rather too quickly, and there were a number of loose ends — the members of the family, for instance — which were not attended to until the theater version.

I had a great deal of trouble getting the idea of this play accepted by a network. The producers of three shows were willing to do it, but only the *Philco Television Playhouse* was able to get its sponsor to agree to the production. I am

170

told that on the show to which I first submitted the idea there was a fierce battle between the producers and the advertising agency as to the desirability of producing a play which poked fun at so much that was gloriously sacred. The official who turned it down, faced by his producer's anger, agreed to submit the story to a number of other people in his agency to get, in the rich phrase of the middleman, "their thinking on it." The entire hierarchy of the agency read *Visit to a Small Planet* and, to a man, rejected it.

It is my dream that one day advertisers will buy only time on the air as they buy only space in magazines: that they will exercise no more control over the programing of a network than at present they do over a magazine's editorial policy. I am quite certain that no big business would allow an advertising agent to supervise the operations of its experimental laboratory. Yet the same business thinks nothing of allowing its agent to be a theatrical entrepreneur, blithely unaware that it takes rather more taste than not to determine good plays from bad, good entertainment from dull; and it is a poignant fact that in the mad race to sell things to the public even the most reflective graduate of the Harvard Business School is apt to lose all sense of the length of art, the shortness of life, even perhaps forget the incongruity of drummers producing plays. As matters now stand, the advertiser is critic, casting agent, producer and, of course, salesman all rolled into one. And, poor creature, he is to be pitied; a single angry housewife in Des Moines can chill a luncheon at Toots Shor's with one illiterate scrawl of rage . . . while, at this very instant, many an ulcer no larger than the tip of a ball-point pen has begun to burn because some cretinous sharecropper has announced that he will never buy another Cadillac because one or another of his fragile moral sensibilities was shattered by a girl smoking a cigarette, or a reference to divorce!

The advertiser must steer his delicate course between the irritable pride of art on the one hand and the blunt exigencies of those reluctant Medicis, the sponsors, on the other. Fortunately, nothing is eternal . . . even Madison Avenue, even television!

Visit to a Small Planet was a happy occasion for everyone concerned: for Jack Smight, the director, for the cast, especially Eddie Andrews and Alan Reed, and of course for the star, Cyril Ritchard, whose performance was perfection and who will re-create the rôle on the stage.

THE
Death of Billy the Kid

Performed July 24, 1955
on
The Philco Television Playhouse (NBC)

Produced by Gordon Duff
Associate Producer: Robert Alan Aurther
Directed by Robert Mulligan

The Cast

BILLY THE KID	Paul Newman
PAT GARRETT	Frank Overton
JOHN POE	Mike Strong
CHARLES BOWDRE	Michael Conrad
SAVAL GUITERREZ	Harold Stone
CELSA GUITERREZ	Muriel Birkson
PETE MAXWELL	George Mitchell
GENERAL LEW WALLACE	Matt Crowley
JOE GRANT	Jason Robart
A DRUNK	Joseph Anthony

Act One

Fade in on a saloon in Ft. Sumner, New Mexico; the year is 1878. In the room — a bar, tables, a pool table — are Charlie Bowdre, a young outlaw; Saval Guiterrez, an older resident of the town; Joe Grant, a heavy-drinking, boastful man; and a drunk whose name no one knows. The Drunk stands nearest the door; he has cadged all the drinks he can from the three men. Sadly, he waits for a newcomer.

GRANT. I tell you one thing: the governor'll have Billy teaching Sunday School when he gets through with him, and that's the truth.

CHARLIE. Not Billy. He's got a long memory.

SAVAL. But the fighting's over now. McSween is dead. Nothing will bring him back, or any of the others gone. *(Proposing toast.)* Well, Charlie . . . Joe, here's to peace in Lincoln County.

CHARLIE. No more Murphys fighting McSweens.

GRANT. In fact there ain't no more Murphys and Mc-Sweens to speak of.

SAVAL. No, nor a lot of others just as fine.

(Pat Garrett, a tall, slow man, a former gunfighter and rancher, enters.)

CHARLIE. Hey, Pat Garrett. Come on over . . . have a drink.

GARRETT. Thank you. Hello, Charlie, Saval . . . Joe. Billy showed up yet?

CHARLIE. He's on his way. You heard the news?

GARRETT *(nods)*. I heard.

SAVAL. Our Billy's a big man now with Governor Wallace himself begging to talk to him. Pete Maxwell just brought Billy the message. The governor's at Lincoln now, waiting on him.

GARRETT. Billy going to see him?

CHARLIE. He ain't said.

SAVAL. Just think! The governor's at Lincoln, waiting on him.

GRANT. Well, it's luck, that's all . . . him so famous when there's a hundred men in the Territory shoot better than him. Men too . . . not green boys.

CHARLIE. Don't let Billy hear you talk that way.

GRANT. I talked that way before he was born, and that's the truth. I got no fear of boys.

CHARLIE. Joe Grant's drinking a lot.

SAVAL. What you doing next, Pat?

GARRETT. Don't know. Maybe start ranching again.

CHARLIE. Going to be dull with no fighting in Lincoln County.

GARRETT. I don't mind one bit. Just as long as I find me a way to live.

GRANT *(bitterly)*. The best shot in the Territory! And all

them stories back East about Billy the Kid: made-up stories, that's what they are! Just because he got luck, because he's shot with it like gold in a hill.

CHARLIE. Keep dreaming, Joe Grant, keep drinking and dreaming . . .

GRANT. I ain't drunk.

(Cut to door as Billy, a blond youth wearing a Mexican sombrero, enters. The Drunk approaches him.)

DRUNK. Good evening, Mr. Bonney. I am a senior citizen of this Territory and an admirer of yours, Mr. Bonney, a great admirer. Will you pause for one instant in eternity . . . *(Billy hands him a coin.)* Thank you, Mr. Bonney.

BILLY. Hello, Pat.

GARRETT. Hi, Billy.

SAVAL. You been with ladies?

GRANT *(sneering)*. Drinking tea with ladies . . .

GARRETT. That's just what he was doing, drinking tea with my cousin Maria.

BILLY. That's right, Pat. I was with Maria, rocking on the porch.

GRANT. Rocking on the porch, playing house . . .

CHARLIE *(to Billy)*. The boys are collecting, like you wanted.

BILLY. You joining us, Pat?

GARRETT. Stealing cattle?

BILLY. Stealing? No, we just pick up these stray heifers and we take them down to Old Mexico to sell. Come on with us. You're the best gun in the Territory.

GARRETT. Second best.

BILLY *(smiles)*. I won't dispute your word.

(Billy crosses to the pool table, starts to play.)

GARRETT. What are you gonna do when you see the governor?

BILLY. I just want to look at him. You know, he's a real general from the war. I never saw a general.

GARRETT. Never saw a governor either.

BILLY. I don't care about them, but a general, now that's something, fighting them Johnny Rebs down there.

GARRETT. You were born the wrong time, Kid.

BILLY. Well, I was born. That's the most a man can ask. You join us, Pat?

GARRETT. No, Billy. I'm sick of trouble.

BILLY. We going to miss you.

(Joe Grant suddenly approaches from the bar.)

GRANT. Billy! I make you a bet.

BILLY. What's that?

GRANT. I bet I kill a man tonight before you do.

BILLY. Who's talking about killing tonight? We're all friends, ain't we?

GRANT *(producing money)*. Twenty-five dollars. Here it is. Now you put up, Billy, unless you're afraid of losing. Saval, you're the nearest one to an honest man. You hold the stakes.

SAVAL. Now, no trouble, please. Joe, forget this bet, eh?

GRANT. Forget this bet? Not with these odds. Why, look at me: betting with the Kid himself, the famous Kid, so famous there's a price on his head.

CHARLIE. You drinking too much, Joe Grant. You starting to dream again.

BILLY *(softly)*. I'll bet, if it makes you happy. Let me see what kind of gun you got.

GRANT *(hands over pistol)*. This old gun's the last thing many a man saw, and that's the truth.

BILLY. It's real fancy. Real fancy. Covered with pearl, too. I like things covered with pearl.
(While Billy examines it, he opens the chamber and, unobserved, slips out two cartridges.)

CHARLIE. Watch out for him, Billy. He's in a mean mood. He's all likkered up.

BILLY. I'll watch out, Charlie. *(Billy returns the gun.)* I'll bet you already got somebody picked out, Joe.
(Billy crosses to pool table. When Billy's back is to him, Grant, with a sudden shout, takes aim and fires, but there is only an empty click. Billy turns and slowly, with one easy gesture, shoots him. Grant falls. There is silence in the saloon. No one moves.)

CHARLIE. He was wanting the reward on your head.
(Saval, without a word, puts the money, the stakes, on the pool table.)

GARRETT. Good thing his gun jammed.

BILLY. Thank you, Pat. *(He opens his right hand and shows the cartridges. He grins.)*

GARRETT. That's a good trick! You couldn't lend me a bit of that betting money, could you? I'm broke again.

BILLY. Sure. Take it all.

GARRETT *(collecting money)*. That Joe Grant was one precious fool.

BILLY *(smiles)*. And that's the truth.

Dissolve to the courthouse room at Lincoln: a table, two chairs, a portrait of Lincoln, two windows and a door. General Lew Wallace, U. S. Marshal Poe and Pete Maxwell, a middle-aged friend of Billy's, are there. It is noon the next day. Poe is at the window. There is a sound of horse's hoofs.

WALLACE. Is that he, Mr. Poe?

(Poe looks out window.)

POE. Yes, General, that's him, riding down the street of Lincoln with his gun on his knee.

(Wallace and Maxwell join Poe at the window.)

WALLACE. He's so young . . .

POE. That trigger finger ain't young.

MAXWELL. You notice, General, there's no one in the street when Billy rides through town. . . . I'd better go bring him up.

WALLACE. All right, Mr. Maxwell.

(Poe starts to follow him.)

MAXWELL *(stops him).* I think it would be wise for Billy to see a friendly face first. Don't you agree, Mr. Poe?

(Poe nods and turns back into room, but Billy is already at the door.)

MAXWELL. Hello, Billy.

BILLY. Hello, Pete. *(To Poe.)* You the general?

MAXWELL. No, Billy, that's John Poe, the U. S. Marshal. *(Leads him to Wallace.)* This is the governor, General Lew Wallace. William Bonney, General.

BILLY. Hello, General.

WALLACE. Mr. Bonney, you . . . you're not what I thought.

BILLY. Well, I left my horns and my tail up in Ft. Sumner.

WALLACE. Will you excuse us, gentlemen? *(Maxwell and Poe leave.)* Sit down. I've heard a lot about you, Billy. The whole country has. The President and I had a long talk about you before I came West.

BILLY. Were you a general of cavalry or foot?

WALLACE. Both. I commanded a division at Shiloh.

BILLY *(nods)*. And you saved Cincinnati from the Rebels. I heard tell about you, and about the war.

WALLACE. Sit down, Billy. *(Both sit.)* Where were you born?

BILLY. New York City.

WALLACE. You came West with your mother when you were a boy. You killed your first man on her account when you were twelve years old.

BILLY *(smiles)*. I guess we both heard about each other.

WALLACE. Yes, most everyone's heard of Billy the Kid.

BILLY. Not all of it's true.

WALLACE. How many men have you killed?

BILLY. Maybe twenty. How many men you killed, General?

WALLACE. That was war.

BILLY. This is war, too.

WALLACE. It was, but it's over now and we're offering amnesty for everyone involved in the McSween-Murphy dispute. I want this to be a peaceful territory.

BILLY. I'm sure it will be, General.

WALLACE. Then you'll help us? You'll settle down?

BILLY. No, sir, I will not. Why, you know what'd happen to

me if I put this gun down? I'd be killed in a day. You watched me riding down that street — I saw you in the window — well, there were guns in windows and doors all up and down that street, just waiting for me to look away.

WALLACE. But if you were to change?

BILLY. They'd kill me just as dead.

WALLACE. You could go West, to California. Start over: a new life, where no one knows you.

BILLY. Would *you* start a new life where no one knows you? No, this is where I'll live as long as I live.

WALLACE. You know you can't stand up to all of us. You have no chance. One man's too small, even Billy the Kid.

BILLY. I never planned on a long life. One day I'll be too slow or there'll be too many . . . but between now and that day I'll live the way I like.

WALLACE. You were fond of McSween, weren't you, Billy? Well, he was an honest man, a brave one.

BILLY. McSween's dead. So are the men who killed him.

WALLACE. I am told he regarded you as his son.

BILLY. Well, I'm an orphan now, General. Sad, ain't it?

WALLACE *(officially)*. William Bonney, do you accept the amnesty offered all who were involved in the Lincoln County cattle war with the understanding you cease violence and obey the law of the United States?

BILLY. No, sir.

WALLACE. Are we to be enemies?

BILLY. I don't see why. I leave you alone in Santa Fe. You leave me be in Lincoln County. *(Wallace doesn't answer.)* Well, I guess I better be going now.

WALLACE. I wish you would help me.

BILLY *(pauses at door)*. You know . . . it ain't such a long way, General, from here to Shiloh.

WALLACE. The distance is no greater than a man's honor. *(Billy looks at him with disgust; then he goes. Maxwell and Poe return.)*

MAXWELL. Well, Governor?

WALLACE. He refuses.

MAXWELL. I told you he would.

WALLACE. We'll need a new sheriff down here. Whom do you propose?

MAXWELL. Pat Garrett.

POE. Isn't he a friend of Billy's?

MAXWELL. We're all friends, but Pat wants a job, and Pat's a great fighter: he's cold, he's hard . . . he's a rock.

WALLACE. Would he shoot his friend if the law required it?

MAXWELL. Yes, Pat would.

WALLACE. Send him to me in Santa Fe. *(He crosses to window. During this we hear horse's hoofs retreating.)*

WALLACE *(softly)*. What a man that boy could be.

> Montage: Billy firing. Pat Garrett in pursuit. The dates 1878, 1879, 1880 are superimposed in quick succession.
>
> Dissolve to the kitchen of Saval Guiterrez's house in Ft. Sumner. Saval and his young wife Celsa sit at dinner as Pete Maxwell enters excitedly.

MAXWELL. Saval! Saval! Saval, they've got him trapped!

SAVAL. Got who?

CELSA. Billy.

MAXWELL. The Kid. Pat Garrett and his men got Billy holed up in an old cabin at Stinking Spring.

SAVAL. As long as he's *in* the cabin they haven't caught him yet.

MAXWELL. He'll never escape. Not now. And they'll hang him for sure.

SAVAL. Are you glad, Pete?

MAXWELL *(startled)*. Glad? No, no, I guess I'm not. Relieved, but not glad. It's like killing a fine hawk who's been raiding your chickens. . . .

CELSA *(nods)*. He *is* like a bird, like a hawk.

> *Dissolve to Garrett and Poe and two men outdoors; it is a moonlit night. All are armed.*

POE. How many do you think there are, Pat?

GARRETT. Four, maybe five.

POE *(nervously)*. We ought to send for more men. We ain't got enough.

GARRETT. We got as many as they got, Poe.

POE. I know, but *he's* in there.

GARRETT. I can handle Billy.

POE *(nervously)*. I'm sure you can, Sheriff. I'm sure you can.

GARRETT. You been reading those storybooks about him? The ones they print back East?

POE. No, but I just hope you know what you're doing, Pat.

GARRETT. I make you a promise. We'll go back to Lincoln with Billy tomorrow — maybe alive, maybe dead — but we'll have that boy slung over a saddle.

> *Dissolve to interior of the cabin. Charlie Bowdre is at one window. Billy at another. Two other men keep watch.*

CHARLIE. Wish we had a fire going in here. Billy, I'm half froze.

BILLY *(grimly)*. If I know Pat, we'll be plenty warm soon.

CHARLIE. You think he'll set us afire?

BILLY. If we let him get near enough he will.

CHARLIE. My hands are turning blue. *(Beat.)* Billy.

BILLY. Yes, Charlie.

CHARLIE. What chance we got?

BILLY. No chance at all I can see.

CHARLIE. Think we ought to give up?

BILLY. And go back to Lincoln and get hung?

CHARLIE *(shudders)*. It's going to be a long, cold night. Wonder how many of 'em there are?

BILLY. Enough. *(To one of the men.)* You see anything?

MAN. No.

CHARLIE. Billy.

BILLY. Yes?

CHARLIE. You know what day this is?

BILLY. I don't keep no track of days, Charlie.

CHARLIE. Well, it's Christmas.

BILLY. Yes, Charlie.

CHARLIE. Well, don't you know about Christmas?

BILLY. Yes, I heard tell, Charlie. Keep your eye on what you're doing.

CHARLIE. When I was a kid we always had a big dinner come Christmas Day. That was on a farm where we lived, nine of us kids, in the South before the war, before we moved West. . . .

BILLY. Charlie, watch what you're doing. There's men moving around out there. They can see you.

CHARLIE. So every Christmas — this is before we came West from Carolina — well, we would all get together just about this time . . .

(A pistol shot. Charlie gasps and falls. Billy crosses to him.)

BILLY. Charlie, I told you . . . now look! You gone and got yourself killed!

CHARLIE. Help me up, Billy. Help me up.

BILLY. What for, Charlie?

CHARLIE. Help me, Billy.

BILLY. There's no point.

CHARLIE. For the love of God, Billy, help me! Let me stand up. I'll be all right standing up. Nobody dies standing up. Billy, Billy, please.

BILLY. All right.

(He helps Bowdre to his feet. He puts a gun in his hand and leads him to the door.)

BILLY *(carefully)*. You're going to help me, Charlie. You're going out there, firing, and you're going to run and you're going to keep running . . .

CHARLIE. Keep ahold of me, Billy. I'm going to fall.

BILLY. You hear me now? You keep running. You keep firing. *(He opens door.)*

CHARLIE. Billy, don't let go of me. Please!

BILLY. Good-by, Charlie.

(He shoves Bowdre out into the night and slams the door. Two gun shots.)

BILLY *(disgustedly)*. He just stood there.

Cut to Garrett and Poe.

186

POE. Which one was it?

GARRETT. Charlie Bowdre, old friend of mine . . . a good boy.

POE. It must be hard for you, hunting down old friends.

GARRETT. They'd do the same to me in my place.

POE. It's a cold night. Think we could have a fire?

GARRETT. No fire till we set the cabin going. (*Shouts.*) Billy, you ready to come out?

POE. He'll never budge.

GARRETT. We'll give him a little while longer. We'll pick off a few more of the gang. None of them's going to slip away in all this moon.

Cut to cabin. Billy is at the window. Beside him is one of his men.

MAN. What do we do now, Billy?

BILLY. Wait.

MAN. They got us holed up proper.

BILLY (*softly*). How I'd love to get me a bead on Pat Garrett. He knows me too well. Oh, Pat, you hold out a little longer, keep the fire off us and when that moon sets . . .

GARRETT (*offstage*). We're setting fire to you, Billy! Come on out!

(*Billy looks at the others.*)

Cut to Pat and his men as the cabin door opens and Billy's two men step out. They are led away. Then Garrett goes cautiously to the door as Billy appears, smiling.

BILLY. Hi, Pat.

GARRETT. Hi, Billy.

BILLY. How you been, Pat?

GARRETT. Pretty good. Except when *you* worried me.

BILLY. Like the new job?

GARRETT. I like being sheriff.

BILLY. The pay pretty good?

GARRETT. Good enough.

BILLY. Then maybe you can pay me back that fifty dollars you borrowed in Ft. Sumner.

GARRETT *(nods)*. I owe you money. I aim to pay you back.

BILLY. Well, we'll be seeing a lot of each other, I guess.

GARRETT. For a while.

BILLY. Then what?

GARRETT. They'll put you on trial in Lincoln.

BILLY. Then what?

GARRETT. Then they'll hang you, Billy.

BILLY *(softly)*. No, no, Pat. You ain't going to *hang* me.

Fade out on Billy's face, still smiling.

Act Two

Fade in on the courthouse at Lincoln, same room as in Act One. Billy, with manacled hands, plays cards with one of his two guards; the other paces the room, talking.

SECOND GUARD. Guess you ain't hearing nothing from the governor, Billy. Guess he ain't writing you even one letter. And if you don't hear from him, why, you'll hang next week, like the judge said. To hear you tell it I thought you was a friend of General Wallace and that's why we been so nice to you. . . . We been real nice, ain't we, Billy? But it looks like he was no friend, because he's paying you no mind, sitting back there in Santa Fe, writing a book. Yes, writing a book is the talk, though that's a peculiar thing, ain't it? Him being a military man and all. Writing a book, while Billy the Kid gets hung.

(He passes his rifle under Billy's chin, but Billy continues to play cards.)

FIRST GUARD. Leave him be.

SECOND GUARD. I was just saying my mind. I figured the governor would do something. Billy kept saying he

189

would all through the trial, claiming . . . what was that thing? Amnesty. *(Crosses to door.)* Well, I'm going on across the street and get me some food.

FIRST GUARD. We'll be here. *(Second guard goes.)* Old Bob talks big.

(The guard rises and crosses to open window. Billy leaps after him and throws his arm chain around the guard's neck. They fall to the floor. Billy takes the man's gun. He aims it. The guard gets to his feet, still stunned, as Billy thrusts his manacled hands at him.)

BILLY. Strike these . . . quick!

FIRST GUARD. It won't do no good. You won't get out of Lincoln alive!

BILLY. You hear me? *(Guard nervously unlocks manacles.)* Now the legs.

(But the guard tries to seize the shotgun. Billy shoots him. The man falls and Billy, his feet still chained, swings out of the window as the second guard runs back into the room; he stops when he sees the body on the floor.)

BILLY *(softly)*. Hey, Bobby.

(Guard looks up. Billy shoots him and leaps over the railing.)

> *Dissolve to Saval's kitchen. Celsa is preparing dinner. Sound of horse's hoofs. Maxwell and Saval enter.*

SAVAL. He's done it, Celsa!

CELSA. I know.

MAXWELL. But how did you hear? He only escaped this morning.

CELSA. I've been told three times already. The first time I heard he'd killed two guards. The second time I heard he had killed two guards and Pat Garrett and set fire to the courthouse. The third time I heard he had killed two guards, Pat Garrett and the governor himself in Santa Fe . . .

MAXWELL. Well, he killed two guards and escaped, still wearing chains on his legs.

SAVAL. Was there ever a boy like him!

MAXWELL. Do you think he'll come here?

SAVAL. No, he'll go down to Old Mexico. . . . And I'm glad.

MAXWELL. So am I. I never wanted him hung. Well, I'd better get home. Celsa, I got a new side of beef over to the house. If you need any, just cross the road and help yourself.

CELSA. Thank you.

MAXWELL. And if you hear any real news of the Kid, let me know.

CELSA. I don't hear news. Only stories from women.

MAXWELL. Well, *adiós pues.*

SAVAL. *Adiós.*

(*Maxwell goes. Saval and Celsa look at one another. Neither is aware of Billy standing in the back door.*)

BILLY. Hi. (*He enters, smiling.*)

SAVAL. Billy! What're you doing here?

CELSA. Come in, Billy.

BILLY. I figured I'd drop by and see old friends. You are my friends, ain't you?

SAVAL (*nervously*). Of course we're friends. But you're not safe. Pat Garrett's only two days' ride from here.

BILLY. I came to see Maria, ask her to take a trip with me down to Old Mexico.

CELSA. Maria's not in Ft. Sumner.

BILLY. No?

CELSA. She's gone to Santa Fe.

BILLY. For how long?

CELSA. A week, two weeks . . . I don't know.

BILLY. Then I'll just hang around, I guess, till she gets back.

SAVAL. You'll stay *here?*

BILLY *(nods)*. Sure.

SAVAL. In this house?

BILLY *(surprised)*. I thought we was friends, Saval.

SAVAL. We are . . . we are, but . . .

BILLY. If you don't want me, I'll go somewhere else.

CELSA. No, you stay with us.

BILLY. Thanks. I'm going to be real quiet for a time. There won't be no excitement.

CELSA. But then?

BILLY. Well, I'll think of something.

SAVAL. Billy, don't. This isn't the old days when it was all right for a man to go killing and stealing because that was the way of the country. It's changed now. You're all alone now.

BILLY. I been alone since the day they killed McSween.

SAVAL. No, I mean people are sick of the killing. They're not with you any more.

BILLY. You against me?

CELSA. Not against *you,* Billy.

BILLY. But you figure I've had my day?

SAVAL. In this Territory, in this part of the West, Billy, you've had your day.
(Billy looks at him for a long moment.)

> *Dissolve to the porch of Maxwell's house in Ft. Sumner. It is a long, low porch with two doors set in the adobe walls. At one end hangs a side of beef. Garrett and Poe appear.*

GARRETT *(calls)*. Pete Maxwell! You home? Anybody home?
(Maxwell appears in a doorway.)

MAXWLL. Oh! Why, hello, Pat . . . John. What're you doing in town? I thought you was chasing around south of Lincoln.

GARRETT. Chasing's the word, chasing shadows in the sun. Pete, we're tired. That Kid's gone like he never lived.

MAXWELL. Well, he's had two weeks to get out of the States. I expect he's in Old Mexico. Sit down. Unseasonable weather for this time of year . . . hot, terrible hot.
(They all sit on a low bench.)

POE. Well, think of us: riding through the desert, day after day, like a bunch of fools, being laughed at in the papers.

MAXWELL. Not laughed at. No one ever thought it likely you'd even catch that boy, much less hold him.

GARRETT. And the people are protecting him. The Mexicans know where he is, but they just smile when we ask — *no comprende, no comprende.* I'm sick of it.

MAXWELL. Well, they're superstitious. They think he's a kind of god.

GARRETT. Do you?

MAXWELL. Me? Of course not. He's just Billy to me.

GARRETT. You wouldn't protect him, would you?

MAXWELL. Why, Pat, I was the one told the governor about *you.* I'm the one helped get you your star.

GARRETT. Would you protect him, Pete?

MAXWELL. I wouldn't want to.

GARRETT. Would you tell me where he was if you knew?

MAXWELL *(slowly).* No. I'd be afraid.

POE. Can we stay the night?

MAXWELL. Of course.

GARRETT. Is Maria Gonzalez here?

MAXWELL. No. She's gone to Santa Fe. You think Billy would come to see her?

SAVAL'S VOICE. Pete!

(Saval appears. He is startled to see Garrett and Poe.)

MAXWELL *(nervously).* Hello, Saval . . . look who just got in town.

SAVAL. Hello, Pat. I heard you was South.

GARRETT. We're looking for Billy.

SAVAL. I know.

POE. You hear anything about him?

SAVAL. No . . . nothing.

GARRETT. Come on, John, let's go over to the saloon.

MAXWELL. I'll have your room ready for you, Pat.

GARRETT. Thanks.

(Garrett and Poe exit.)

MAXWELL. Where's Billy now?

SAVAL. At the saloon.

MAXWELL. The saloon? But you just heard Pat. He's going there now.

SAVAL. There's a lookout posted.

MAXWELL *(marveling)*. The whole of Ft. Sumner's protecting him!

SAVAL. But for how long?

> *Dissolve to bar. Billy sits at a table alone*
> *as the Drunk joins him.*

DRUNK. Good evening, Mr. Bonney. I saw you sitting alone and I wondered if I might have the pleasure of your company.

BILLY. You mean a drink?

(He pushes bottle toward the Drunk, who sits down, pours himself a drink.)

DRUNK. You're very kind, Mr. Bonney. May I drink a toast to your health, sir? *(Drinks.)* That was good. I must say I needed that. Very bracing, very bracing indeed. . . . Mr. Bonney, I have followed your career with much interest.

BILLY. Everybody has.

DRUNK. I saw you first when you were sixteen.

BILLY. Where was that?

DRUNK. At McSween's house. I was visiting there. I had just come West to . . . to seek my fortune.

BILLY. *You* knew McSween?

DRUNK *(with dignity)*. I wasn't always . . . immoderate in my habits.

BILLY. I wish McSween was alive right now and sitting just where you are.

DRUNK. He was a fine man. He thought you would be a fine man too some day. *(Sighs.)* Oh, it was terrible the way things turned out: the fighting with Murphy . . .

all over nothing, some foolish misunderstanding for which the two great houses, Montague and Capulet, went to war . . .

BILLY. Who?

DRUNK. Challenging one another upon the plains of heaven while the angels wept.

BILLY. You're drunk.

DRUNK. Am I? Well, in a single less lofty phrase: it was too bad. Too bad they fought, too bad men died, too bad about Billy the Kid.

BILLY. Why too bad about me?

DRUNK. Because you'd have been an honest boy; but having to fight changed you, like a dog who goes wild when he tastes blood and reverts to the wolf he was in ancient times.

BILLY. You been reading them storybooks.

DRUNK. Well, you *are* the story, the golden boy marked for slaughter.

BILLY. You think so?

DRUNK *(softly)*. Oh yes, I see the end of it already.

BILLY. Will it be soon?

DRUNK. Soon, my dark angel . . . soon. Might I trouble you for another libation? *(Drinks.)* I was there, Billy, the day you ran from the burning house of McSween, when only you were chosen to survive that day. And now there's just you left, still at war.

BILLY *(nods)*. Just me.

DRUNK *(stretches)*. I feel when I drink that I could do anything, be anything . . . even be you.

BILLY. That's not much.

DRUNK. Oh, but it is! To be a name on the lips of men. There is nothing so sweet. . . . Tell me, Billy, did you ever kill anyone you loved?

BILLY. Only people I had to, people I didn't know most times.

DRUNK. You never tumbled a god from his temple, did you?

BILLY. I don't understand your talk.

DRUNK (*grandiloquently*). Blind in the city of Gaza, I shall destroy the temple.

BILLY. You talk too much, old man.

DRUNK (*stung*). *Old* man! You pity me, don't you?

BILLY. I don't feel nothing about you.

DRUNK (*rises*). Oh, you are marble. You don't love. You don't hate. Mr. Bonney, I am not old. I am not an object of pity. I have *chosen* to live as I do, to dream as I do. It is a choice, deliberate and proud. Be warned.
(*The Drunk departs, passing a Mexican boy who enters and claps his hands: the signal. Billy exits through the back door. Garrett and Poe enter bar.*)

GARRETT (*to the bartender*). Two shots.

BARTENDER (*sets them up*). Good to see you again, Pat.

GARRETT (*to Poe*). He's in this town somewhere. (*To the bartender.*) You seen Billy?

BARTENDER. Billy who?

GARRETT (*grimly*). And that's the way it's been.
(*They drink; they leave the bar.*)

   Cut to the street. The Drunk approaches.

DRUNK. Good evening, gentlemen. (*The two men pass him by.*) Mr. Garrett!

(Poe starts to go on but Garrett pulls him back. They go to the Drunk.)

DRUNK *(smiling).* Good to see you in Ft. Sumner again.

GARRETT. Have you seen him?

DRUNK *(innocently).* Who? Who is that?

(Garrett removes a bag of coins from his belt and holds it up to the Drunk's gaze.)

GARRETT. There's a reward for information.

POE. A big reward.

DRUNK *(suddenly horrified).* No! *(He starts to bolt, then he stops of his own will.)* It would be a brave thing for me to do in this town, wouldn't it?

GARRETT. Yes, it would. Try to be brave!

DRUNK. Oh, I will. I will! I see you underestimate me, too. Well, listen to *me.* Listen while *I* talk, while *I* bring him down!

(He whispers to Garrett and Poe. We hear only the word "Saval." Then Pat and Poe leave him and go down the street. The Drunk sits on a bench and spills the money out of the bag. He starts to leave it . . . a terrible struggle . . . then, fearfully, he gathers the money and runs with it down the street.)

Fade out.

Act Three

Fade in on the kitchen of the Guiterrez house where Garrett, Poe and Celsa are gathered. It is an hour after the previous scene, early evening.

GARRETT. We know he's been staying here, Celsa. People have seen him. People have talked.

CELSA. Do you see him? I don't.

POE. Mrs. Guiterrez, there is a reward for him. Big money.

CELSA. You must be eager to collect it.

GARRETT. Where is Billy?

CELSA. I don't know.

GARRETT. He was here. He was staying in this house.

CELSA. Well, he is not here now.

GARRETT (*carefully*). Celsa, we've all known each other a long time. We're like a family, but even in a family there's got to be some law, some justice. You must give him up.

CELSA. To you?

GARRETT. To the law.

CELSA. No, it's not the law you want him for, Pat . . . it's for yourself.

GARRETT. For myself?

CELSA. Because you're afraid of him, because he is all that you would like to be, because you think by killing him *you'll* be the larger man, but you won't. People are not as simple as you think. They know why Pat Garrett wants Billy the Kid.

GARRETT. I am the sheriff. It is my duty to see that laws are obeyed.

CELSA. Duty, but not your pleasure.

POE. She's crazy.

GARRETT. He was like my own brother, like a son, but like a father it is my duty to punish him.

CELSA. And who will punish you?

POE. Come on. She won't talk.

GARRETT. I will punish myself.

CELSA. In your dreams?

GARRETT. Dreaming or waking, it's all the same, but I mean to find him.

(Saval enters.)

SAVAL. What are you doing here, Pat?

POE. We know Billy's staying with you.

SAVAL. Who told you that?

POE. Is it true?

SAVAL. No.

POE. Come on, Pat. We'll learn nothing here.

SAVAL. But *if* he was staying here he wouldn't come back, not with you in Ft. Sumner.

POE. We'll find him. You tell him that when you see him.

SAVAL. If I see him.

POE. I'm sure you will.

(Poe and Garrett start to door, Garrett pauses, turns to Celsa.)

200

GARRETT. It's only chance has made it like this.

CELSA. Believe what pleases you most. It's all the same.

GARRETT (*fiercely*). Tell him to go, if you love him. Tell him to go *now*.

(*Pat Garrett and Poe leave.*)

SAVAL. Who told them?

CELSA (*shrugs*). I have a feeling they'll meet very soon, Pat Garrett and Billy.

SAVAL. And that'll be the end of Pat.

CELSA. Who can say what will happen when those two meet again?

> *Dissolve to the porch of Maxwell's house.*
> *Maxwell and Billy are together.*

MAXWELL (*urgently*). . . . or even Santa Fe's safer than here.

BILLY. No, not Santa Fe, nor Old Mexico . . . just Ft. Sumner, that's all I want. Right now, anyway.

MAXWELL. Pat's got his suspicions. I'm sure of it.

BILLY. *You* wouldn't be telling him, would you?

MAXWELL. You know me better than that, Billy. But a hundred people know you're here. Someone's going to tell him.

BILLY. He still has to catch me. (*Sighs.*) Look at that old red sun going down. Hot day tomorrow, I reckon.

MAXWELL. I'll sell you a good fast horse cheap.

BILLY (*grins*). Why, Pete, you know I never *buy* me a horse.

MAXWELL. You're giving me palpitations of the heart, your staying here so open. Suppose Pat rode up right now. What would you do?

BILLY. I'd say, "Hello, Pat," and I'd blow his head off.

MAXWELL. Look! My hands are shaking. I'm not a young man, Billy.

BILLY. I'm sorry, Pete. *(Deep breath.)* Oh, I even love the dust in the air and the smell of frijoles cooking in the town.

MAXWELL. But the country's changing, Billy. It's not what it was.

BILLY. The people maybe but not the air and the moon rising yonder . . . and there's the first star.

MAXWELL. You're not going back to Saval's, are you?

BILLY. Don't know yet. There's talk Pat's gone back to Lincoln.

MAXWELL *(nods)*. He left me over an hour ago.

BILLY. I know.

MAXWELL. How did you know?

BILLY. I hear things. Pat hears all about me and I hear all about him. You know, the Mexicans say I can see through an adobe wall.

MAXWELL. Well, if he's gone back it's not for long.

BILLY. Look, how red the moon is. . . .

MAXWELL. We need rain bad this spring.

BILLY. How quick night falls! Well, I think I'll walk a bit. So long, Pete.

MAXWELL. So long, Billy.

> *Dissolve to the bar. Garrett and Poe are there, alone.*

POE. Sometimes I wonder if he's real or if we haven't thought him up to plague ourselves with.

GARRETT. He's real, and he plagues me.

POE. That time we caught him I kept wondering to myself: Is this Billy the Kid? This young boy? Is this the worst killer in the West? Twenty-one men lying under the ground because of him? I couldn't believe it and that's why I think sometimes — you know, a crazy thought — that we made him up, that there's no such person.

GARRETT (*suddenly*). We ain't going back to Lincoln tonight.

POE. But you said you were. They're expecting us.

GARRETT. We're going to stay the night.

POE. What's got into you?

GARRETT. If I don't find him soon, I'll bust. Oh, I pray this is the night!

> *Dissolve to Guiterrez kitchen. Billy and Celsa are in the kitchen.*

CELSA. Saval won't be back till late.

BILLY. You mind if I stay a while?

CELSA. I wish you wouldn't.

BILLY. It's all right. Pat's left town.

CELSA. Even so.

(Billy stretches out on the floor.)

CELSA. Billy, do you feel you been bad?

BILLY. I don't think about it.

CELSA. It is not right to kill.

BILLY. Well, it's right to live and I wouldn't be living if some other people hadn't died along the way.

CELSA. Not always. There were times when it wasn't necessary when you went ahead anyway like a wild animal, killing for the sport . . .

BILLY. Don't start on me, Celsa. I got no ear for preaching.

CELSA. I won't say nothing.

BILLY. I'm sleepy. *(Celsa dims the lamp. Moonlight pours through the window. Billy suddenly sits up.)* Celsa, you ever read one of those books they write about me?

CELSA. Yes, once.

BILLY. I always meant to read one of those books. It must be funny, reading about yourself doing fool things people think up in their heads. *(Pause.)* Say, how do those books end, Celsa?

CELSA. You live happy ever after.

BILLY. I like that kind of storybook.

CELSA. Why do you stay here?

BILLY. I'm waiting, that's why.

CELSA. Waiting for Maria Gonzalez?

BILLY. Waiting for her.

CELSA. I think you're waiting for Pat Garrett.

BILLY *(drowsily)*. Yes, I'm waiting for him, too.

> *Dissolve to Maxwell's porch. Poe and Garrett approach.*

POE. Pete! Pete!

(Maxwell appears in his night clothes.)

MAXWELL *(nervous)*. And here I was thinking you boys had left town. Well, come on in and stay the night.

POE. Hope you don't mind, Pete.

MAXWELL. Not at all. It's just . . . unexpected.

POE. Pat here had a sudden brain storm about staying on this night.

GARRETT. If you don't mind, Pete.

MAXWELL. No, no, not at all.

GARRETT *(to Poe).* Wake me in two hours. And you, Pete, you stay close by me.

> *Dissolve to the Guiterrez kitchen. Celsa is at the table reading her Bible in the half-light of the lamp as Saval enters. Billy is still asleep on the floor.*

CELSA *(whispers).* Hush, he's asleep.

BILLY. No, he's awake. *(He stands up.)* I'm hungry. Hello, Saval.

CELSA. I can only fix you frijoles.

BILLY *(to Saval).* Pat Garrett leave town?

SAVAL. Gone to Lincoln, they say, but he'll be back.

BILLY *(to Celsa).* Just beans?

CELSA. That's all.

BILLY. You know, I been dreaming about that side of beef over to Pete Maxwell's.

CELSA. I'll get you some.

BILLY. No, I'll go. You want any, Saval?

SAVAL. No, no, thanks, Billy.

(Billy has crossed to the open door.)

BILLY. Look, it's almost light as day.

SAVAL. Be careful, Billy.

CELSA. I'll go start the fire.

> *Billy goes out as we dissolve to Maxwell's porch. Poe sits smoking in the moonlight. Billy approaches stealthily. He moves up to the porch, not seeing Poe. Poe gives a start*

> *but doesn't recognize him. Billy leaps back against the wall.*

POE. Who is it?

> *(As Poe approaches, Billy turns quickly into the dark doorway. He pauses, sensing there is someone in the room.)*

BILLY *(draws gun)*. Quien es?

> *(Two shots ring out and Billy, shot head on, staggers back onto the porch and falls, gun in one hand, knife in the other. Poe stands over him, bewildered, as Maxwell and Garrett emerge from the room. Maxwell lights a lantern.)*

POE. It's Billy!

GARRETT. I knew it was him when I heard his voice!

> *(Maxwell examines the body.)*

MAXWELL. Shot through the heart, shot dead!

POE *(excited)*. And you outdrew him, Pat, you outdrew Billy the Kid!

MAXWELL. In the dark.

> *(People appear — Saval, Celsa, the Drunk, the bartender, Mexican women — all have heard the shots. When they see who is dead, they murmur among themselves and the women weep.)*

CELSA. I knew it would end like this.

> *(Maxwell and Poe have placed Billy on a bench on the porch. He lies there now, arms crossed like the effigy on a tomb. Garrett stands over him, looking down.)*

DRUNK *(to no one)*. This was the night the temple fell.

> *(The weeping and the murmuring grow louder. Poe turns to Garrett.)*

POE. What's wrong with these people? Don't they know what he was? Listen to them, you'd think you had shot a saint.

MAXWELL. They loved him.

POE. Well, now they'll love Pat Garrett. Now he's the hero. He's the best man of us all.

MAXWELL *(softly)*. It was dark and Billy had no chance.

POE. What do *you* say, Pat?

GARRETT *(slowly)*. Say? I say I have killed Billy the Kid, and there's nothing more.

Fade out on Billy's face in the moonlight.

The Death of Billy the Kid, though by no means the most admired of these plays, is my favorite. I believe that the development of the story disturbed a number of critics because it is not usual to compose a play in which the denouement is implicit in the title itself. But I was aiming, no doubt inaccurately, at tragedy and I wanted a massive effect, a passionless inevitability which, I believe, all things considered, the play's production achieved.

There is an odd problem which I have encountered time and time again as a writer and as a reader, as a playwright and as an audience: *people do not listen to words.* This is due perhaps to habits acquired in everyday life, where conversations are dependent not so much upon the use and the arrangement of words and ideas as on certain familiar tones of voice, gestures, hesitations. Anyone who has listened to an actual conversation reproduced on a tape recorder will notice immediately that people seldom complete sentences as they talk, that often a tone of voice or a key word is sufficient to communicate intention. For a playwright who is interested in language, this is always disturbing and, in a sense, it explains the continual popularity of low-keyed, stereotyped plays and movies where the audience feels immediately at home because no scene will ever surprise it, ever turn out to be different from its initial anticipation. For example: sophisticated man takes unsophisticated ingénue to a sidewalk café; it is her first visit to Paris. He offers her Pernod; she drinks it; she makes a face; she coughs. This scene has been done thousands of times. Dialogue is not necessary. The audience does not need to listen as it watches the familiar action; the audience has a cozy sense of being home.

Now, one is not so vain as to demand rapt attention from an audience which after all wants only to be entertained; nevertheless, one does expect from the more literate audience a closer attention to what is actually said rather than what they think is said as they watch a scene develop. They assume everything will be entirely familiar and, when it is not, when they detect an unanticipated phrase or response, they are apt to feel uneasy, obscurely cheated.

I suspect that the more severe reactions to *The Death of Billy the Kid* were due to the fact that I took an American legend already done many times by the movies at a fast pace and deliberately slowed it down, directing my attention — and the audience's — to the moral implications of this boy's life, to the essential tragedy in the Greek rather than in the Hollywood sense.

Some years ago, I planned a novel about William Bonney, but because I lack the patience to be a scholar I could never assemble the information I needed in just the way I would need it if I were to do justice to such a theme. Yet I never lost interest in Billy and, finally, television afforded me the opportunity to re-create him.

I knew exactly what I wanted to do with the legend, but Billy himself proved a considerable problem: How to show him? What, after all, could one say about a cold-blooded little killer who, in the words of a noted psychiatrist, was "an adenoidal moron"? I could not in all honesty make him an introspective human being aware of the startling design he was creating in a crude new world which needed all the idols fate might bring to people that pantheon which each nation is forever building to house its gods, its demons and its central men. Billy was precocious, as the nation was, ruthless, as the nation was and still can be. Despite the cruelty of his ways, there was something in him which struck fire in the imagination of others and those who knew him realized early in his progress that he was not ordinary, that he was meaningful in a way few men are; that the meaning was essentially dreadful was a problem only to the reflective man. His appeal was to those deeper emotions which he evoked by the mere fact of existing.

My decision, finally, was to show not so much Billy himself as the people who created the myth of Billy the Kid. There was the obsessed friend turned agent of the law, Pat Garrett, driven by pride to measure himself against a hero, to become the hero by destroying him — like the

King of the Wood in *The Golden Bough.* And then there
was the Drunk, who wallowed sensuously in the melodrama, quite willing to play Judas if that was the only rôle
available in the company; General Wallace, appreciative
of the legend but a man of state who must tidy up no matter what; and all the others who wanted to partake of the
story. Were these figures in actual life the way I re-created
them? I should think not. I was in pursuit of the myth, not
the fact, and only the bare incidents of the play are true
in the historic sense. The real truth to me was that a boy
inadvertently had become a legend. At a certain time and
in a certain place a youth who would now be a mere sta-
tistic, a figure on the graph of juvenile delinquency, became, through some poetic alchemy, part of a nation's
dream of itself — not unlike that shady financial manipula-
tor, George of Cappadocia, who became, no doubt to his
own posthumous surprise, Saint George, the killer of the
dragon and the patron saint of England.

The cast which played *The Death of Billy the Kid* was
unusually fine. Paul Newman managed, with discretion
and power, to interpret a nearly impossible rôle: he had to
be, simultaneously, both wicked mortal and potential god-
ling. Joseph Anthony's performance as the Drunk was wonderful: he caught the bravura style of the character without himself stumbling into the florid and excessive. Bob
Mulligan directed with great delicacy and I can think of
no play I have written which so moved me in the actual
performance, and I may say, parenthetically, that I am
neurotically aware of my own faults as a dramatist: every
badly written line reverberates like thunder in my head

when I hear it spoken by an actor. In Gordon Duff's production of this play I was barely aware of my own faults and that indeed is magic. The notable meagerness in the characterizations as I wrote them will, I hope, in the proposed film be replaced by that ideal drama one has always in one's head: the thing accomplished fully, that impossible perfection which so tantalizes. The television play was only a forty-seven-minute blueprint of a work yet to be done properly.

In the first two years I wrote for television, I adapted many books and plays. Except on the *Philco-Goodyear Playhouse* it was always, at least for me, a singularly dreary business getting an original play produced in a form acceptable to me as well as to the buyer. I dislike writing treatments, those pidgin-English outlines which are expected to record in detail the incidents of an unwritten play. Unluckily for me, I never know what a play is going to be like until it's written and I am suspicious — certainly envious — of a writer who knows in advance what his play is going to be: easier, I should think, to divine the nature of an unborn child. But, alas, not illogically, most programs want a full description of what they are to buy and this description must be read, in ascending order, by the producer, by the network, by the advertising agency and, finally, by that shadowy eminence, the sponsor, from whose lair, generally deep in the Midwest, inscrutable ukases are issued, mysterious but binding ordinances calculated to confound and quell his producer, not to mention that fragile vessel, the playwright. It was often, I found, simpler to accept for adaptation a book or play which the mad Midwestern troll had already decided should be dramatized than embark on an original project. And adapting is not uninteresting. Aside from the basic talent for making a play, an adapter must possess certain small gifts of which the most important is, very simply, knowing how to read. Surprisingly enough, most playwrights, no matter in what medium they work, are seldom literary men and more often than not they are indifferent to writing which is not for the stage. This of course is a stunning generality, which I shall not defend other than to remark that for some unfathomable reason I have known more playwrights than any other single group and I have found all but a few easily bored with the slow, dense order of the novel, additional proof, to my mind, that prose plays are not literature, that the means of their composition and execution are unlike the novel in every sense. A virtue in one is often a fault in the other. This fundamental difference accounts for some of the extraordinary adaptations offered on television and in the movies. For myself, though I have had some remarkable failures as an adapter, I have always tried at least to convey the precise essence of the work at hand. When I have failed, it has been as a dramatist not, I like to think, as an interpreter.

There are certain works peculiarly difficult to adapt and one is not always conscious at first of what is dramatically viable. Certain themes, certain *seemingly* possible works do not transfer easily from the page to the camera. For instance, when I adapted *A Farewell to Arms* I was reasonably pleased with the script. Hemingway is the scenarist of the novel. His scenes are direct and taut. So playable does he seem that for the first time as an adapter I used actual dialogue from the novel. I was particularly confident that the first love scene in the hotel bedroom would play beautifully. Well, it did not. Hemingway's dialogue, so theatrical on the page, does not fit easily into the mouths of actors. It is prose dialogue, not stage dialogue, and though the eye cannot always distinguish the difference, the ear does, mercilessly. Despite Diana Lynn's delicate performance as Catherine, we failed, and I have yet to see a faithful adaptation of Hemingway either on television or on the screen which was as good, in its way, as the original. On the other hand, William Faulkner, considered obscure by the impatient, was much easier to adapt.

Eva Wolas, the story editor at *Suspense,* asked me, shortly after *Dark Possession,* if I should like to adapt "Smoke." I said yes, believing she meant Turgenev's "Smoke." Faulkner's "Smoke" is a complicated mystery story — to this day, I am unsure as to who was where at what time. But fortunately Faulkner had provided, as he nearly always does, even in his *Saturday Evening Post* potboilers, a strong emotional conflict: two brothers who have fallen out with their father and with one another. The scene between them at the end of Act One was, I think, exciting in every sense, and a particular triumph for the director, Bob Mulligan. Later that season we worked together on another Faulkner story, "Barn Burning."

Often the most famous works are disappointing to adapt because both public and reviewers are used to earlier versions. I thought the dramatization we did on *Climax* of *Dr. Jekyll and Mr. Hyde* was a good one, but unhappily our audience was more interested in the transformation than in the argument of the play. Michael Rennie's Hyde was not as horrendous as his movie predecessors and the audience, conditioned by those movies, felt cheated. It did no good to say that Hyde was never meant to be a physical monster. Ideally, for television, Hyde's face should never be shown. The audience, however, wanted tusks and we failed them. One critic found the girl I'd created unlike the girl in the original story (remember Miriam Hopkins's bare leg swinging over the side of the bed? Ingrid Bergman's tremulous singing?). I was tempted to point out that the only girl in Stevenson's story was under twelve, but there is no point in correcting any popular variation on a classic theme; the movies have made this philosophic melodrama into a Grand Guignol fairy tale and any attempts to go back to the original are unwise violations of the familiar.

Adapting plays is a much easier task than adapting works of prose. In the case of an old play like Royall Tyler's *The Contrast*, the first American comedy, I merely edited, cutting away a long subplot involving comedic servants, concentrating my focus on the principals, only occasionally trimming their speeches. After the dress rehearsal, Henry Steele Commager, who was to introduce the play on *Omnibus*, pointed out to me with some asperity that the subplot I had blithely discarded contained the one character for which the play was famous: Jonathan, the Yankee servant. But Jonathan was a great bore and, looking back, the play was a bit of a bore too, though the production was noble. I was even freer with Ferber and Kaufman's *Stage Door* (the play, not the movie so well remembered and so different from the original). Our production was notable for Miss Rhonda Fleming, the movie star, who is very tall with red hair and for whom we provided a sly scene beside a swimming pool. Miss Fleming played this scene beautifully. She also maintained a classic calm when Victor Moore began to plunge about in the last act, muttering, "What the hell am I doing here in the middle of the night?" to the alarm of the network.

With *Smoke* and *Barn Burning* I have included *The Turn of the Screw*, my favorite adaptation and one of the best productions I have seen on television (these wreaths I heap upon my own plays are not entirely self-congratulatory; rather, they are in recognition of the collective nature of dramatic writing — in this case, Henry James's story, my adaptation, Paul Feigay's production, Seymour Robie's direction, the performances of Geraldine Page, Rex Thompson and Cathleen Nesbitt, not to mention the scenery, lighting, music, camera work, all contributing to a success for which I was, roughly, one eighth responsible).

I was extraordinarily pleased when *Omnibus* asked me to adapt the story. Like everyone else, I had my theory about the governess. I had always felt that the ghosts of the servants existed for her alone, that the children had been corrupted by the *living* servants, not by their ghosts. The governess, whose own delicate balance was unsettled by her charges, by the house Bly, by the imminence of evil, suffered hallucinations which were to her so real that she communicated them in turn to the children — in short, she frightened Miles to death. James himself is ambiguous as to the reality of the ghosts. He had obviously intended to write a fantasy but he was, after all, too firmly rooted in the reality of the actual world, too devoted to the precise use of his own massive psychology to permit magic. As a result, Mrs. Grose cannot see the ghost the governess sees, the ghost Flora denies seeing. Even at the end Miles cannot see what it is the governess commands him to look upon in the dark. These are, finally, *her* ghosts, *her* folly, not theirs. The real shadow is evil done, evil unforgotten. That, in brief, is the line I took in my adaptation, differing considerably with many honorable predecessors.

Smoke

From the story by William Faulkner
Performed May 4, 1954
on
Suspense (CBS)

Produced by Martin Manulis
Directed by Robert Mulligan

The Cast

GAVIN STEVENS	E. G. Marshall
YOUNG RAINEFORD	Pat Hingle
VIRGINIUS	Bart Burns
GRANBY MARDIS	George Mitchell
JUDGE DUKINFIELD	G. Albert Smith
DOC WEST	Kenny Delmar

Act One

Fade in on the cemetery of a Southern town. It is a late summer evening. An old man, Raineford Holland, is smashing a gravestone with a shovel. His horse is tethered to a nearby tree. Young Raineford, his son, a thick-set youth in overalls, appears, crosses to him and tries to take away the shovel. The old man strikes him. They fight grimly.

Dissolve to a photograph of Raineford Holland as Granby Mardis, a lean, pious man, arranges black crêpe around it. The photograph occupies the place of honor over the mantel of Granby's shabby Victorian parlor. He steps back, regards his handiwork gravely as Virginius, Raineford Holland's other son, a somber man of thirty, enters and, without a word, his expression unchanged, crosses to the mantel, picks up the photograph, black crepe and all, and hurls it to the floor, where it breaks. Granby is appalled.

GRANBY. Virginius! He was your father! *(He kneels and collects the glass.)* And now you've gone got broken glass all over the floor.

VIRGINIUS. There'll be no mourning in this house, Granby.

GRANBY. We got to do the right thing.

VIRGINIUS. Not while I'm here.

GRANBY. This is my house, Virginius.

VIRGINIUS. Then I'll go.

GRANBY. Oh, now don't you carry on, Virginius, we're friends, ain't we? Blood cousins. . . . Least we can do is show proper respect for our dead. . . . They're burying him tomorrow and you and me are going to the funeral, even if we go alone. . . .

VIRGINIUS. You bury him alone.

(Virginius pushes Granby aside.)

GRANBY. That's un-Christian.

VIRGINIUS. He threw us all out. He ruined the land. Let him die alone.

(He starts to go when the front doorbell rings. Granby goes to open the door, talking fast.)

GRANBY. We got to do the right thing. People are talking. You know how they talk. They say old Raine . . . I mean, your father . . . they say he didn't meet with no accident.

VIRGINIUS. His horse threw him and he broke his stubborn head.

(Judge Dukinfield enters.)

DUKINFIELD. Virginius . . . Mr. Mardis . . .

GRANBY. Come right in, Judge. We were paying our respects to old Raine, now gone to his reward.

DUKINFIELD. No doubt a rich one. Excuse me for dropping in like this. . . .

GRANBY. We appreciate your gesture, Judge Dukinfield . . . in our bereavement.

DUKINFIELD. I came to ask you, Virginius, if you know where we can find your brother Raine.

VIRGINIUS. Back in the hills, I guess. I wouldn't know. We don't speak, Raine and me.

GRANBY. What do you want him for, Judge?

DUKINFIELD. Old Raine's will. I'm going to probate it Monday. All the heirs got to be on hand. You, Virginius, and you too, Mr. Mardis.

GRANBY. Me? An heir?

DUKINFIELD. In a small way. (*Virginius leaves the parlor abruptly.*) Nobody can say Virginius is grieving.

GRANBY. He's deep. He don't show his feelings. (*Dukinfield starts to the door.*) I hear they're saying old Raine wasn't thrown from his horse. They say, when he was killed, he was in the field, defacing the tombstones of all his relations, his wife's family. And *then* it was the horse threw him, *if* it did.

DUKINFIELD (*noncommittal*). Fine horse. I sold it to him. Well, good afternoon, Mr. Mardis.

GRANBY. Can't offer you anything, can I, Judge?

DUKINFIELD. No, thank you. I have an appointment with Gavin Stevens.

GRANBY. Well, drop by anytime.

(*Dukinfield leaves the room. Granby steps into the doorway and looks after Dukinfield.*)

SMOKE

Dissolve to Doc West's General Store. Doc West is behind the counter. A number of customers shop idly. A fan stirs the heavy summer air. Gavin Stevens, a dapper, amiable-looking man, leans against the counter, drinking Coca-Cola.

DOC WEST. Now come on, Gavin, just because you're County Attorney you don't have to be that close-mouthed. *(Lane, a young man in a double-breasted suit, comes up to counter.)* You know what I mean. Old Raineford Holland was murdered there yesterday sure as . . .

LANE. Package of Monograms, please.

DOC WEST. Monograms? We don't carry that brand. No call for it down here. You from the North? *(Begins to rummage.)*

LANE. St. Louis. Well, if you don't have Monograms . . . *(He turns to go.)*

DOC WEST. Now hold on a minute: I think sometimes I got two of everything back here. And here we are: two packs of Monograms. *(He comes up with two packages of cigarettes.)* But I think I ought to warn you, they're kind of old.

LANE. That's all right.

(Lane pays him and leaves as Dukinfield enters and motions for Stevens to join him by the door. Stevens does; Doc West looks after them curiously.)

STEVENS. I was looking for you, Judge. I was just down to your office.

(Dukinfield sits on an upturned crate.)

222

DUKINFIELD. I was looking for you, too.

STEVENS. That office of yours is ten degrees hotter than downtown at noon.

DUKINFIELD *(chuckles)*. Well, gives some of my clients an idea of what's in store for them. Only thing I mind is all that tobacco smoke they puff at me, rests right on the floor for days.

STEVENS. Rumors are really flying, Judge.

DUKINFIELD. That so?

STEVENS. You think one of the two boys did it?

DUKINFIELD. Hard to say.

STEVENS. Well, one thing's for sure: there's nobody in Jefferson not pleased. Old Raine was the worst man in these parts and that's a considered opinion. But of course you and I, Judge, we got to be above prejudice. We got to serve the law and, besides, we don't want to appear suspicious because maybe nothing's wrong after all. Maybe it *was* his horse threw him. . . . You think he was murdered, don't you, Judge? *(Dukinfield nods.)* Virginius? Or young Raine?
(A phone rings at the counter. Dukinfield rises, takes Stevens's arm and together they cross to the door.)

DUKINFIELD. I'll tell you something strange, Gavin. You ever see that horse? The one they *say* threw old Raine? Well, I happen to know . . .

> *Dukinfield and Stevens go. Cut to Doc West at the counter as he answers the phone.*

DOC WEST. Yes, he's here. *(Calls.)* Judge! Judge! *(Into phone.)* No, he just left. Guess he's gone to the courthouse. . . . Young Raine's in town? You really see him? He was what? Carrying a gun!

Dissolve to Granby's parlor, that evening, after dinner. Granby and Virginius are in their shirtsleeves. Granby is reading a Bible. Virginius is cleaning his rifle. The lights in the room are dim. From another place can be heard, faintly, the sound of a radio. There is a feeling of heat, of tension in this night.

GRANBY *(suddenly)*. Terrible . . . terrible funeral. They kept away from us like we bore the plague of Egypt.

VIRGINIUS. It was a funeral, Granby, not a revival meeting. . . . I don't know where the dirt comes from. I clean this gun last month and now it's all clogged up.

GRANBY. You think he'll come *here*, Virge?

VIRGINIUS. My brother? Why should he come here?

GRANBY. Well, you're heirs together, ain't you? Now the big place is both of yours . . . though they say your daddy left it only to you.

VIRGINIUS. He had to leave it to one or the other of us, that's what Mother's will said. She didn't know he'd go spoil it all.

GRANBY. Why did he hate the land so? I never could understand . . . the best acres in the county and he let them idle.

VIRGINIUS. Why does a man hate anything?

GRANBY. Pride, says this book. Pride which . . .

(Young Raine has appeared in the doorway, carrying a shotgun.)

RAINE. Pride which goeth before a fall.

SMOKE

(Granby gasps and leaps to his feet. Virginius does not look up but continues to clean his gun.)

VIRGINIUS. Come in, Brother.

GRANBY *(frightened)*. Sit . . . sit down, Raine.

VIRGINIUS. You come to quarrel?

RAINE. No. My quarreling days are done.

GRANBY. You go out to pay your respects to your daddy? To the cemetery?

RAINE. You're getting the land, ain't you, Virge?

VIRGINIUS. I reckon some of it'll be mine.

RAINE. All of it.

VIRGINIUS. No, you'll get your share.

RAINE. I don't want any part of that land.

VIRGINIUS. By rights half should go to you and half you'll get whether you want it or not.

GRANBY. He's right. It was all your mother's once, until your father showed up out of nowhere and married her.

RAINE. Bringing the devil with him.

VIRGINIUS. He's dead now. And it's over, all the hating.

RAINE *(softly)*. Not while *we* live.

VIRGINIUS. And what would you mean by that?

RAINE. You took his side against me when we came of age, when I asked for my share of the farm.

VIRGINIUS. You said you didn't come to quarrel.

RAINE *(suddenly contrite)*. I . . . I been living too long alone.

VIRGINIUS. You can go back to living in the big house, if you want.

RAINE. No, I'll stay alone in the back country. I ain't fit for the world.

VIRGINIUS. Why did you come here tonight, Raine?

225

RAINE. To see if you'd split with me, if you got the place. To talk. . . .

GRANBY *(quickly)*. Virge is a man of his word.

(Virginius has finished assembling his rifle. He slips a bullet in it, cocks it; Raine releases the safety on his gun.)

VIRGINIUS *(again)*. Why did you come here tonight, Raine? *(The doorbell rings. Raine looks through the door.)*

RAINE. It's Gavin Stevens.

VIRGINIUS. I'll tend to him. . . . You want to go?

RAINE. No, I got no place to go.

(Raine sits down beside his brother as Granby lets Stevens in.)

GRANBY. Good evening, Mr. Stevens.

STEVENS. Good evening, Granby. Mr. Holland. . . . And the *other* Mr. Holland.

GRANBY. Make yourself at home.

STEVENS. I'll just be a minute. I drove out from Jefferson to tell you there'll be some official questions asked tomorrow. We'll want all three of you there at the courthouse.

GRANBY. What for?

STEVENS. Judge Dukinfield was shot this afternoon. *(He turns to go.)* I want you three gentlemen to be there.

> *He leaves, shutting the door softly behind him. Virginius and Raine look at one another, in league at last. Only Granby appears shocked. Fade out.*

Act Two

Fade in on Judge Dukinfield's office the next morning. There is a desk at one end of the room and a long table with chairs in the center. Gavin Stevens is alone. He goes to the desk and thoughtfully picks up a heavy metal box. He opens it. Then, taking a long puff on his pipe, he blows smoke into the box and slams the lid shut. He returns the box to its place on the desk; then he crosses to the door, opens it and addresses the officer on duty.

STEVENS. Show them in.

(Doc West and other grand jurors enter. They murmur hello to Gavin and take their places in the chairs around the table. Virginius, Granby and Raine enter together. The brothers sit together. Granby sits next to Stevens.)

STEVENS *(looks about pleasantly)*. All here? Good. Now we'll start.

DOC WEST. We're here to talk about Judge Dukinfield, ain't we?

STEVENS *(nods), And* the Holland will . . . and the death of Raineford Holland.

VIRGINIUS. There a connection?

STEVENS. There's a connection, Virginius. The same man who killed old Raineford Holland is responsible for the death of Judge Dukinfield in this very room.

VIRGINIUS. Let's hear your "connection," Gavin.

RAINE. Yeah. We're waiting on you, Mr. Stevens.

STEVENS *(crosses to the brothers)*. Our story begins with your father, who came here fifty years ago and married your mother, Cordelia Mardis . . . through her he got the Mardis plantation.

VIRGINIUS *(softly)*. You have any other news for us?

STEVENS. A lot of news, Virginius. Be patient. I'm speaking for the record now. Your mother died. Your father got the land. He didn't like you boys and you didn't like him. First, he drove out you, Raine; then, a few years ago, he broke with Virginius, who went to live with Mr. Mardis here, a cousin. . . . Virginius, why did you quarrel with your father?

VIRGINIUS. None of your business.

STEVENS. This is a murder inquiry. Answer the question.

VIRGINIUS. Because he was wrecking our land deliberately. Because he hated us and he had to leave the land to one or the other of us when he died. He wanted to leave us nothing. So he let the land go bad.

STEVENS. That was a condition of your mother's will — that you boys inherit?

VIRGINIUS. You wrote it. You ought to know.

STEVENS. That's right. I've done all the Holland wills. By the way, your father's will, the one the Judge was fixing to probate, leaves the estate to you, Virginius . . . you know that?

VIRGINIUS. In a general way.

STEVENS. There're no other bequests . . . except a dollar to Granby Mardis . . . to buy a prayer book with: the old man wanted to remember him for taking Virginius in.

GRANBY *(bitterly)*. One dollar!

DOC WEST. What's all this got to do with the Judge being murdered?

STEVENS. Don't rush me, Doc. We got to go slow. We got to be careful. You see, the murderer is sitting in this room.

DOC WEST *(alarmed)*. Well, okay, be careful, Gavin.

STEVENS *(amused)*. I will. Now I want you all to think back on the last few years, on old Raine living alone, his sons waiting for him to die, think of him, half mad, ruining his land, breaking the tombs of his family out of spite . . . and now think of the man who killed him. Think of the man who followed, or met, old Raine in the field that day, who beat him to death and then put his foot in the stirrup to pretend he'd been dragged by his horse.

DOC WEST. How do you know all this, Gavin?

STEVENS. Because the man made a mistake . . . he forgot something he should've known, something Judge Dukinfield knew, and was murdered because he knew it: that horse, when struck, *wouldn't bolt,* that horse would lie down when he was struck, as everyone close to old Raine knew. As Judge Dukinfield knew because he sold the horse to Raineford Holland.

DOC WEST *(puzzled)*. So you think old Raine beat his horse and it lay down on him?

229

STEVENS. No. Somebody else. A man who could wait fifteen years for his chance . . . and then make a mistake and recall it too late, spending several bad days and nights wondering what the Judge would do, knowing the Judge would find out that he'd done murder, to get the land for himself . . . knowing the Judge had it all figured out. *(Stevens has crossed during this to Virginius.)* So what do you think, Virginius?

RAINE *(abruptly)*. You're wrong.

STEVENS *(turns)*. Where am I wrong?

RAINE *(rising)*. Because *I* killed the old man. *(A startled murmur from the jurors.)* But it wasn't on account of the farm. And I didn't lay a hand on the Judge. Now bring on your sheriff.

STEVENS *(softly)*. No. *You're* wrong.

RAINE *(fiercely)*. You're a liar. I told you. I found him in the cemetery. He was there like I heard, breaking my mother's tomb, like he broke her life. I thrashed him and I left him lying there *and he was dead.*

STEVENS. No, Raine, he wasn't dead. He was unconscious. You see, someone else came along *after* you and finished the job.

DOC WEST *(confused)*. What're you trying to tell us, Gavin? Who did what?

STEVENS. Raine, do you smoke?

RAINE *(startled)*. Smoke? No.

STEVENS. You smoke, Virginius?

VIRGINIUS. No, none of us ever did.

STEVENS. What about you, Granby?

GRANBY. No, sir, I never use it.

STEVENS. A clean family record.

DOC WEST. You out of your mind, Gavin?

STEVENS *(to Doc West)*. Yesterday I was at your store. While I was there a city fellow driving a funny little European car stopped and came in and asked for a Northern cigarette, a kind you had only two packages of, and them pretty old. But the city fellow bought a pack. . . . Now someone I know saw that funny little foreign car parked out behind Virginius's barn yesterday, a few hours before Judge Dukinfield was killed.

VIRGINIUS. Go on. . . .

GRANBY. Oh, *that* fellow. He came to see *me*. He wanted some of these little built-up horses for this . . . this game . . . polo. I didn't have nothing for him and he went on. Virginius knows . . . he was right there all the time. Fellow was a stranger. . .

(But Stevens has turned away and gone to the desk.)

STEVENS. We all know one of the peculiar things about this room is there's not much ventilation. And the tobacco smoke, it banks up on the floor and stays there couple days at a time. . . . Guard. *(He turns to the guard at the door.)*

GUARD. Yes, sir?

STEVENS *(indicates box on desk)*. Where was this metal box when you found the Judge?

GUARD. On the floor. I shut it and put it back on the desk.

STEVENS. Thank you. Now whatever's shut up in a metal box will remain unchanged *longer* than if it was in a wooden box. For instance, you can shut up smoke in a box with a tight lid like this one and a week later it'll still be in there and a chemist or a tobacco seller, like Doc West over here, he can tell what kind of smoke it its . . . especially if it's a strange brand of smoke, a kind we don't have much of in Jefferson, maybe only two packs of, one of which was sold to that stranger . . . that city fellow named Lane we picked up yesterday.

(Granby makes a sudden lunge at Stevens and knocks the box out of his hands. It falls to the floor. The lid opens: a faint wisp of smoke curls from the interior and Granby, on his knees, hysterically fans the smoke away.)

GRANBY. It's gone! You got no evidence!

STEVENS. We got this, Granby. And we got you. *(He holds up pistol with silencer. Granby tries to pull away; the guard holds him.)*

GRANBY *(hysterically)*. That's not my gun. I don't own a gun.

STEVENS. That pistol belonged to Lane, the fellow who came to see you, who told us the whole story when we picked him up: how you hired him from St. Louis to kill the Judge. You figured with Raineford Holland dead and with Virginius soon to be dead . . .

VIRGINIUS. With me what?

STEVENS. First the old man. Then you, Virginius. He was going to take care of you next; then, him being your heir, he would inherit the farm. Poor Granby, everything went wrong and now that farm's never going to be yours.

GRANBY. But it should've been mine. They had no right to it. None of them. None of the Hollands. That was Mardis land. My family's land; *mine* by rights. But I tell you one thing: I'd do it again, I'd kill every last Holland on earth to get our land back.

(Stevens motions to guard, who leads Granby away. Excited talk in the room as the jurors leave. Virginius starts to go; then he looks back at Raine, who smiles shyly. Together, they cross to Stevens, who is lighting his pipe.)

VIRGINIUS. Gavin, how did you figure about that killer, about Lane? You really catch him?

STEVENS. In a way. He was killed driving north of here, speeding. One of my boys found the gun on him. Gun with a silencer. Then I heard Lane had been to visit Granby. That was all. I didn't have a scrap of proof Granby was connected with the killings so I had to trap him. *(He taps the metal box.)*

RAINE. Gavin?

STEVENS. Yes?

RAINE. One thing bothers me . . . you talked right smart about chemistry and smoke and so on. Well, how did you know there *was* smoke in that box? If you looked to see if it was the right kind it'd blow away. And if it wasn't the right kind, well, Granby would've been safe.

> *Stevens only grins. Then, as the camera moves in tight on his face, he draws on his pipe and exhales. Fade out on the smoke.*

Barn Burning

From the story by William Faulkner
Performed August 17, 1954
on
Suspense (CBS)

Produced by David Heilweil
Directed by Robert Mulligan

The Cast

ABNER SNOPES	E. G. Marshall
BOY	Charles Taylor
JUSTICE OF THE PEACE	James Reese
MAJOR DE SPAIN	Peter Cookson
MRS. DE SPAIN	Beatrice Straight

Act One

Fade in on the boy Snopes outside the country store. He is blond, blue-eyed, dressed in torn coveralls. There is a babble of angry talk from inside. He approaches cautiously. We cut to the inside of the store. Trial is in session. The justice of the peace is also the store owner. He is a middle-aged man, harassed and weary. Abner Snopes, forbidding and grim, stands accused. Harris, an elderly farmer, denounces him to the justice. The boy, meanwhile, has quietly entered and squatted down behind the crowd near the door.

JUSTICE. Quiet! Quiet! *(Bangs gavel; silence.)* Now what proof you got, Harris?

HARRIS. Proof? Three times his hog got in my corn. First two times, I brought the hog back, telling him to fix his own pen.

JUSTICE. When was this?

HARRIS. Month ago, beginning of April. Third time . . . no, *second* time I took his hog back I said, "Here,

237

Snopes, here's some wire, you take it and you fix your own pen and you keep that hog out of my corn."

JUSTICE. Did he?

HARRIS. He did nothing. Nothing at all. So the third time I put that old hog in *my* pen and when he come for it I told him he could get it back when he paid me a dollar pound fee. That night it was when this fellow come.

JUSTICE. You mean Snopes here?

HARRIS. No, some stranger, sharecropper. Never saw him before. He come to my house. He said, "Snopes say, 'Wood and hay can burn.'" *(Crowd murmurs.)* My barn was burned to the ground that night.

JUSTICE. Quiet! Quiet please! You know where this fellow is? The one who brought you the message?

HARRIS. I told you: he was strange to me. I don't know what become of him.

JUSTICE. But that's no proof, Harris. I'm sorry, but . . .

HARRIS. Get that boy up here. *(Turns, points to the boy.)* He knows. There he is! That's Snopes's boy. Come up here, you!

JUSTICE. Come here, boy. *(Young Snopes gets up and approaches cautiously. He stands next to Snopes.)* What's your name?

BOY. Colonel Sartoris Snopes, sir.

JUSTICE. Colonel Sartoris, eh? That's a great name in this country. With that name you can't tell a lie, can you?

BOY. No, sir.

JUSTICE. Where's your mother, child?

BOY. She dead.

JUSTICE. You live alone with your pa?

BOY. Yes, sir.

JUSTICE. Harris, you really want me to question this boy?

HARRIS *(disgusted)*. No. It won't do no good. Get 'em out of here, both of them. I'm sick of the sight of them.

JUSTICE *(relieved)*. Case closed. You're safe this time, Snopes. But I got some advice for you: leave this country and don't come back. Understand?

> *Snopes and the boy turn and leave. Cut outside as two boys attack the Snopes boy, shouting, "Barn burner!"*

BOY *(as he fights)*. He ain't . . . he ain't!

(The justice breaks up the fight.)

OLDER BOY. Dirty barn burner!

BOY *(to justice)*. He ain't, I tell you. And he's brave in the war. Pa! *(His father approaches grimly.)* Tell 'em about the war, Pa, and the Germans, and the medal you got.

> *But Snopes takes the boy, without a word, by the arm and crosses out. Cut to the justice and Harris.*

HARRIS. He was guilty . . . sure as I'm standing here.

JUSTICE. I don't doubt it. But we had no proof.

HARRIS. He drifts from farm to farm, hiring out, causing trouble. He got a dishonorable discharge in the war . . . tried to kill an officer, they say. And I'm telling you he burned down my barn!

JUSTICE. Well, he's leaving town. That's the last we'll see of him.

HARRIS. It better be.

Dissolve to Snopes's truck in the woods. The boy, chewing bread, steps out of it, looks around. Cut to Snopes at the fire as the boy joins him.

SNOPES. You would've told them, wouldn't you?

BOY. Told 'em?

SNOPES. At the court. You were fixing to tell them.

BOY. No, I wasn't. I wasn't saying nothing.

SNOPES *(points with burning stick)*. Blood's all you got. Blood's all there is. You hear me?

BOY. Yes.

SNOPES. You know what I'm saying?

BOY. Blood's all there is.

SNOPES *(menaces boy with stick)*. Your kin, your own blood, that's all that counts in the world and don't you forget it . . . we're both of us alone. Those fellows back there, they knew I got them beat. But they wanted to use you against me . . . against your own blood. And you was going to tell them, wasn't you? *(Grabs the boy's wrist.)*

BOY. No, Pa. I wasn't, honest.

SNOPES *(releases wrist)*. Get in the truck! *(He puts out fire with the coffee.)*

Dissolve to moving truck: Snopes driving, boy beside him.

BOY. Where we goin', Pa?

SNOPES. We're leaving the county. There's this man near Jefferson, name of de Spain. I made a contract with him. We'll live on his farm till harvest.

BOY. He got a house for us to live in?

SNOPES. We stay in the truck. We take nothing from nobody . . . just our share of the crop.

BOY. He live a long ways from here?

SNOPES. Fifty miles maybe . . . just south of Jefferson.
You recollecting what I told you?

BOY. Yes, Pa.

SNOPES. You better. You got no other kin in this world but
me.

> *Dissolve to the porch of the de Spain*
> *house, a handsome porticoed affair, at the*
> *moment being swept by the housekeeper.*
> *Major de Spain comes out on the porch.*

HOUSEKEEPER. Good mornin', Major . . . goin' to be warm
again today.

MAJOR. Yes, looks like it, Lula.

(The major goes. The housekeeper continues her sweep-
ing. Snopes and the boy appear. Snopes passes her and
knocks on the door.)

HOUSEKEEPER *(offended)*. What you want here?

SNOPES. Where's Major de Spain?

HOUSEKEEPER. He not home.

(She opens the door and goes in. Before she can shut it,
Snopes pushes past her into the hall.)

SNOPES. Get out of my way.

HOUSEKEEPER. You get out of here! Miss Anne! Miss Anne!
(Mrs. de Spain comes down the stairs. She is a good-
looking woman, still young.)

MRS. DE SPAIN. Comin'! *(She joins them.)* Yes, Lula, what
is it?

HOUSEKEEPER. I told him Major wasn't here. I told him to
go away.

MRS. DE SPAIN. Who are you? What do you want?

SNOPES. I come to see your husband. I got a contract with
him. I'm Abner Snopes.

MRS. DE SPAIN. Well, he's not here. You'll find him at the
barn.

(Snopes looks at her stonily; then he turns hard and, de-
liberately, on his heel, grinds dirt into the rug; then he
marches out of the house, the boy following him.)

MRS. DE SPAIN *(runs to door).* Hey! Come back, you! *(Then*
she turns and examines the rug.) Lula, look what he
did! To my new rug . . .

HOUSEKEEPER. I tried to stop him, Miss Anne, but I just
couldn't, him staring at me with those mean devil eyes.

MRS. DE SPAIN. He did it deliberately, too. You'd better
call Major de Spain. He's at the south barn. Tell him
the new man's here.

HOUSEKEEPER. Yes, Miss Anne.

> *Dissolve to a clearing in the woods where*
> *the truck is parked. The boy is collecting*
> *wood as the angry major appears.*

MAJOR. Hey, boy, come over here. *(The boy approaches*
him warily.) What's your name?

BOY. Snopes, sir.

MAJOR. Where's your father?

> *Cut to Snopes, who is working on the car's*
> *motor.*

SNOPES. Somebody looking for me?

(De Spain and the boy cross to him.)

MAJOR. I'm Major de Spain. You're the new man, aren't you? Abner Snopes?

SNOPES. That's right. I come to see you this morning, but you wasn't home.

MAJOR *(unfolds rug).* You did this?

SNOPES. Maybe so.

MAJOR. Well, you're going to clean it, Snopes, and the next time you come to my house you come to the back and you wipe your feet. Hear me?

SNOPES. I hear you, Major.

MAJOR. Now report to my foreman. He'll show you your section. You'll find him at the south barn. *(Turns and marches off.)*

BOY. He sure was mad, and all over a dumb old rug.

SNOPES. Stuff like that means a lot to his kind. Well, set the water boiling. *(Smiles.)* I'll clean his rug for him.

> *Dissolve to the hall of the de Spain house.*
> *A knock at the door. The housekeeper an-*
> *swers it. Snopes, rug in hand, accompanied*
> *by the boy, is there.*

HOUSEKEEPER. Major say for you to go round the back way.

SNOPES. Tell him I got his rug for him, all nice and clean.

HOUSEKEEPER. Now you go around . . .

(The de Spains appear.)

MAJOR. That you, Snopes?

SNOPES. I got your rug for you.

MAJOR. So soon? Well, thank you.

(Snopes gives the rug to Mrs. de Spain.)

MRS. DE SPAIN *(as she unfolds the rug).* Oh, no! He boiled it in lye!

MAJOR. You wrecked it, didn't you? You wrecked it deliberately.

SNOPES. No, I did like you say.

MAJOR. Snopes, this is a very valuable rug. It's worth a hundred dollars. Now I know you haven't got a hundred dollars and unless you turn thief you'll never have that much in your life. *(Snopes turns to go but the major stops him.)* Pretty pleased with yourself, aren't you? Well, when harvest comes I'm going to keep twenty bushels of corn out of your share. That'll almost pay for this rug.

SNOPES. Twenty bushels, you say?

MAJOR. Twenty bushels . . . to teach you manners, Snopes.

SNOPES. But we got a contract, Major, you and me. It don't say nothing about your keeping twenty extra bushels.

MAJOR. Then we'll take it up with the judge at Jefferson. *(He goes inside and slams the door after him. Snopes stares at the door a moment.)*

BOY. But that ain't fair, Pa. Twenty bushels . . . that's crazy.

SNOPES. He's got to go to court first.

BOY. We won't give him nothing, will we, Pa? We don't owe him nothing for that rug.

SNOPES. Harvest ain't till October. This is May.

BOY. He can't take it away from us, can he?

SNOPES. I don't see how. *(He strikes a match with his thumbnail.)* But if he does . . .

(He grins at the boy over the flame of the match. Then he drops the match and walks on. The boy, alarmed, stamps it out carefully. Then he runs after his father.)

Act Two

Fade in on the truck in the clearing as Snopes prepares to go to town. The boy watches him.

SNOPES. No, you're not coming! You stay right here. I'll be in Jefferson the whole day.

BOY. Why can't I go?

SNOPES. Because you can't.

BOY. There goin' to be another trial?

SNOPES. He won't get nothin' out of me for that rug of his. *(Mimics.)* "This is a very valuable rug. It's worth a hundred dollars."

BOY. Let me go, Pa.

SNOPES. No. And keep away from that house of thieves. You hear me?

(The boy jumps on the truck but Snopes starts it and he falls off.)

BOY. Pa! Pa! Give him the twenty bushels!

Dissolve to the porch of the house. The boy appears; he looks around, impressed. Mrs. de Spain approaches, carrying flowers. The boy retreats.

MRS. DE SPAIN. Come here, child. Are you afraid of me?

BOY. No, ma'am.

MRS. DE SPAIN. I saw you yesterday and the day before looking at the house. Did you want something?

BOY. No. I was just lookin'.

MRS. DE SPAIN. At the house?

BOY. It's pretty.

MRS. DE SPAIN. Thank you. Come on inside while I fix these flowers. We're having a party tonight. Don't be frightened. (*She smiles and takes his hand. Awkwardly he follows her.*)

> *Cut to the hall. Mrs. de Spain arranges flowers in a vase. The boy looks around him with wide eyes.*

MRS. DE SPAIN. How old are you?

BOY. Eleven. (*Touches picture frame.*) That real gold?

MRS. DE SPAIN. Just gilt.

BOY. Like fool's gold maybe?

MRS. DE SPAIN. Something like that. Do you like living in that old truck with your father?

BOY. We live there most of the time. (*Points to barometer.*) What you use that for?

MRS. DE SPAIN. To tell the weather. It's a barometer.

BOY. What's the weather going to be?

MRS. DE SPAIN (*gaily*). Fair and warmer. (*Pause.*) Where's your mother?

BOY. Dead, since I was little. (*He stares at a sofa.*)

MRS. DE SPAIN. Go ahead, sit down. (*They both sit down.*) You always lived with your father?

BOY. Except when he was in the Army and I stayed in a home. He was a hero. He was real brave. He killed two hundred men and they give him a medal and a piece of ribbon with these little red, white and blue stripes. You got any kids?

MRS. DE SPAIN. No.

BOY. Guess they all growed up, huh?

MRS. DE SPAIN. No, none at all, ever. *(Pause.)* We have an empty cabin down back of the barn. You and your father could live there.

BOY. He likes the truck, ma'am.

(Major de Spain enters. Boy jumps to his feet.)

MAJOR *(at door).* That the Snopes boy?

MRS. DE SPAIN. Yes. We've been having a nice visit, haven't we, child?

BOY. Yes'm.

MRS. DE SPAIN. He's been telling me all about his father, in the war. About the medal they gave him.

MAJOR. A special guardhouse . . .

MRS. DE SPAIN. John!

MAJOR. I'm sorry. *(To boy.)* But your father gave me a bad morning. I had to go up to Jefferson on his account.

MRS. DE SPAIN. What happened?

MAJOR. We saw Judge Dukinfield . . .

BOY *(rising).* He didn't burn nothing! He didn't.

MAJOR. Burn? Of course he didn't burn it. He boiled that rug in lye, that's what he did.

MRS. DE SPAIN. What did the Judge say?

MAJOR. Ten bushels of October corn I keep out of his share, and he let Snopes off with a warning.

BOY. It wasn't much of a rug.

MAJOR *(laughs)*. Well, *we* liked it. Now you scoot.

BOY. Yes, sir.

MRS. DE SPAIN. Come back and see me.

BOY. Yes'm. *(Leaves.)*

MRS. DE SPAIN. He's a nice child.

MAJOR. Looks like a little savage.

MRS. DE SPAIN. It's not his fault, living like an animal in the back of a truck.

MAJOR. You and your stray cats!

(They cross toward stairs.)

MRS. DE SPAIN. And that father of his . . . did you see his eyes?

MAJOR. I could've blacked both of them this morning. Why, the way he talked to me and the Judge, you'd've thought he owned creation.

MRS. DE SPAIN. John, he frightens me.

MAJOR. Well, I expect I frightened him today.

> *Dissolve to the truck that night. Snopes is filling cans with gasoline.*

BOY *(approaching)*. What you fixing to do?

SNOPES *(grimly)*. Ten bushels of October corn, they say. Ten bushels they'll never see.

BOY. Don't do it, Pa. Not to them.

SNOPES *(dangerously)*. You forget what I told you? About kin?

BOY. No, but ten bushels ain't so much and maybe he'll forget come harvest.

SNOPES. He'll remember me when it's time for harvest.

BOY. The lady . . . she was nice to me today.

SNOPES. I told you not to go there! *(He slaps the boy.)*
You got no business there! Oh, he spoke like I was dirt
in front of that judge. Nobody living talks to me that
way. *(Pause.)* I wonder if there'll be enough. You go to
the stable. There's a can near the door, on the left. Fetch
it here and if anybody sees you . . .

BOY. No.

SNOPES. No? *(Grabs the boy hard.)* You forget what I tell
you? You forget? You're my blood . . . all your life
that's what you are! Now get in the back of that truck
and wait till I come back. If I catch you out of there,
why, you won't have no life to live.

> *He forces the boy into the front of the
> truck. Then he picks up the wadding, the
> tins of gasoline and starts off toward
> the barn, camera with him. As he passes the
> house, he pauses and listens to the sound of
> laughter, of music, inside. He smiles grimly
> and crosses to the barn door.*
>
> *Cut to the boy as he gets out of the car
> and runs after his father.*
>
> *Cut to the inside of the barn where
> Snopes has already started the fire.*
>
> *Cut to the barn door as the boy appears;
> he sees the blaze but not his father. He turns
> and runs toward the side door of the house.
> He knocks on the door but no one hears; a
> party is in progress.*

*Cut to the portico where guests are chat-
ting. He rushes past them, into the house.*

*Cut to the hallway where Major de Spain
finally stops him. Mrs. de Spain and the
other guests listen, appalled.*

BOY *(breathless)*. Major . . . Major . . . barn! The barn!
MAJOR. What's the matter, boy?
BOY. It's your barn . . . he's burnin'! You got to stop him!
MAJOR. Stop who?
BOY. Pa! He's burnin' it down.
MAJOR. Hold that boy! *(To the men of the party.)* Come on!
   *(The major takes a pistol from a drawer and crosses to
   the side door, followed by the men.)*
MRS. DE SPAIN. John, be careful!

*Cut to the barn door as Major de Spain
and four of the guests run inside. Horses
whinny. Smoke swirls within. Snopes, unobserved, slips out of the barn and shuts the
door, locking the men inside.*

*Cut to the inside of the barn as de Spain
and the others realize what has happened;
they pound on the door.*

MAJOR. Open that door, Snopes! Open it! *(As he shouts, he
cocks his pistol.)*

*Cut to the outside of the door. Snopes still
stands at the door, smiling. He is still there
when the pistol is fired three times. Holding
his chest, Snopes staggers off toward his*

251

> truck as Mrs. de Spain and the ladies of the
> party come out of the house. Mrs. de Spain
> opens the barn door. The major and the four
> men emerge.

MAJOR *(to the men).* Come on . . . around to the other
side. Get the stock out first!

> *Cut to the truck as Snopes, with great
> effort, crawls into the driver's seat. For a mo-
> ment, he sits, looking straight ahead, and
> then, as though exhausted, he falls forward
> on the wheel, dead, his body pressed
> against the horn, which suddenly blares out
> and continues to sound until the boy ap-
> proaches and gently pulls his father back
> into the seat. The horn stops. The boy, aware
> now that his father is dead, steps back with
> horror. Mrs. de Spain joins him. She puts
> her arm about him.*

MRS. DE SPAIN. Come away, child, don't look.
BOY. I told him not to . . . not to you. *(He buries his face
in her arms.)* He was brave . . . he was real brave.
MRS. DE SPAIN. I know . . . I know.
BOY. He killed these men in the war and they give him
this medal . . . and a piece of ribbon.

> *She comforts him as he weeps. Behind
> them in the car firelight flickers on Snopes's
> dead face. Fade out.*

The Turn of the Screw

From the story by Henry James
Performed February 13, 1955
on
Omnibus (CBS)

Produced by Paul Feigay
Directed by Seymour Robie

The Cast

GOVERNESS	Geraldine Page
MRS. GROSE	Cathleen Nesbitt
MILES	Rex Thompson
FLORA	Nina Reeder
UNCLE	Robert Goodier

Fade in on the study of the uncle's house in Harley Street, the 1880's. The uncle is middle-aged. The governess is intense, young, expectant. We hear her voice narrating as the scene begins.

GOVERNESS'S VOICE. He was a most impressive man on first meeting and I thought myself in luck that day in Harley Street when I sat opposite him in his study and he told me about the children I was to take care of.

UNCLE. A long trip. Mostly business. South Africa. Can't be bothered, won't be bothered. Do you understand?

GOVERNESS. I believe so, sir.

UNCLE. You are colonial, aren't you?

GOVERNESS. Yes, sir, from Canada. I stay now with my uncle in Norwich.

UNCLE. I don't mind colonials. Not in the least. You were highly recommended . . . you know that?

GOVERNESS. I do my best, sir, always. A boy *and* a girl?

UNCLE. Yes, a boy and a girl. My late sister's children. I'm their only relative.

GOVERNESS. Do they live here, too, in London?

UNCLE. No, they're at Bly, in Kent. I keep them there all year round. Whole house to themselves. I'm sure you'll do. You'll find them bright children. The house is comfortable and you will handle everything . . . *every-*

255

thing. A free hand. Don't write to me. Don't bother me. . . . Use your own judgment.

GOVERNESS. Sir, this is a most grave responsibility . . .

UNCLE *(rising).* It is, isn't it? *(She rises.)* I shall be back in the spring. I'll visit you then, at Bly. Good day.

GOVERNESS. Good-by, sir. *(She turns and goes.)*

> *Dissolve to picture of Bly, a large pseudo-Gothic house. We hear her voice narrating.*

GOVERNESS'S VOICE. I saw the house first on a winter's day. A wonderfully comfortable *modern* house with its own park and its own lake. On every side there were signs of the master's taste, of his solidity and good judgment. It was my dream of a house, of home.

> *Dissolve to the entrance hall, stately but comfortable. The two children run down the steps, followed by the governess.*

GOVERNESS'S VOICE. The children were even better than I'd hoped. From a governess's point of view they were enchanting: easy, quick, endearing. They knew instinctively how to please, how to get around me if they chose. Flora was nine years old.

> *Cut to Flora. All three are now in the drawing room, talking, laughing beneath the narration. The drawing room is airy, spacious, with French windows.*

GOVERNESS'S VOICE. Her whole life had been spent at Bly. She had no memory of her parents. She'd been cared for by a succession of governesses and by Mrs. Grose, the housekeeper.

Cut to Mrs. Grose, an elderly woman who enters from the hall. Cut to Miles.

GOVERNESS'S VOICE. Miles, at eleven, was a perfect gentleman, enormously patient with me and seldom patronizing, despite the weakness inherent to my sex. He arrived for his holidays from school the day I came to Bly. And he charmed me with his beauty, quite carried me away in fact, and largely because of him, my first weeks in that house went swiftly, delightfully, in spite of sunless days and the sharp winter wind.
(The children burst out laughing.)

GOVERNESS. Why, Miles, that's not fair! Not fair at all!

MILES. But of course it is. Two starfish and one boat together make . . .

FLORA. She got it all wrong! Oh, Mrs. Grose, it was the funniest thing! Tell her, Miles, tell her!

MRS. GROSE. You can tell me later, Master Miles. Now it's time for your suppers. Off with you.

GOVERNESS. And fix your hair, Flora . . . the way I showed you. It's exactly like a bird's nest now.

FLORA. Really? What sort of a bird?

MILES. A large disagreeable vulture with a great *huge* beak!

FLORA. Oh, Miles! Don't be awful!
(The children run from the room.)

GOVERNESS. You were quite right, Mrs. Grose. They *are* angels.

MRS. GROSE. I've been with them seven years and I've not seen their like. Never could understand why *he* wouldn't take more interest.

GOVERNESS. Their uncle?

MRS. GROSE. Yes. Always off traveling somewhere. Comes here but once a year, and then never complains . . . imagine!

GOVERNESS. You'd rather he found fault?

MRS. GROSE. At least he could show he was interested. Oh! Here's a letter for you, from Miles's school, I should think.

GOVERNESS. It's addressed to Miss Jessel.

MRS. GROSE. She was the governess before you, miss. I've told you about her. You can open it.

GOVERNESS. She died, didn't she?

MRS. GROSE. Yes. Poor silly woman.

GOVERNESS. Poor? Silly?

MRS. GROSE. I shouldn't've said that. Dr. Cousins only last Sunday reminded us we should say nothing but good of the dead, or at least hold our tongues.

GOVERNESS. Now that is hardly fair, Mrs. Grose, to have me bursting with curiosity. Also, I should know everything about my predecessor. I don't want to make her mistakes.

MRS. GROSE. You won't make *her* mistakes, I assure you, miss.

GOVERNESS. You're like the Delphic oracle. I must interpret everything you say.

MRS. GROSE. I suppose I *should* tell you. Before others do. But it was an ugly story, very ugly.

GOVERNESS. Then I'm surprised I wasn't told it in London.

MRS. GROSE. The Master don't like trouble, so we kept it from him. Also it involved rather a pet of his, a valet he picked up somewhere . . . not a proper sort of man at all . . . full of the devil, with an eye for young girls and other wickedness. He drank.

GOVERNESS. Do you mean that the valet and Miss Jessel . . .

MRS. GROSE. I do. It was shameful. She fell in love with him. Imagine, a gentle-born girl like her with . . . with a monster!

GOVERNESS. A monster! That *is* intriguing. And all this here, at Bly.

MRS. GROSE. It was horrible! He was cruel to her. She wept on my shoulder many a time for love of him.

GOVERNESS. Did the children . . . I mean, were *they* exposed to all this?

MRS. GROSE. Who can tell how much children know? The man was always with Miles. They'd go hunting together. I disapproved but I'm only the housekeeper. It's not my place to criticize.

GOVERNESS. What happened finally?

MRS. GROSE. The man — he was called Peter Quint — was killed last spring.

GOVERNESS. Really? How did that happen?

MRS. GROSE. He was coming home late from the tavern. He lost his footing, they say, in the old quarry — it was a misty night. He wasn't found till morning.

GOVERNESS. And Miss Jessel?

MRS. GROSE. Went home to die. A weak heart, they said.

Broken heart, I say . . . just like in the stories . . .
only this time it was better broke than whole, if you
ask me, hard thing as it is to say.

GOVERNESS. What a terrible story! And in this house. It
hardly seems possible.

MRS. GROSE. So I've looked after Flora since spring, while
Miles was away in school.

(Governess glances now at the open letter in her hand.)

MRS. GROSE. Miles will be going back next week. I hope
I'll have all his mending done for him. I don't know
how he . . . what's the matter, miss?

(The governess looks at her, suddenly appalled.)

GOVERNESS. He's *not* to go back.

MRS. GROSE. To the school?

GOVERNESS. They don't want Miles at the school again.

MRS. GROSE. But . . . but why?

GOVERNESS. Well, I . . . I don't know. It says that he is
a "bad influence." What on earth do you think they
mean?

MRS. GROSE *(exploding)*. Nonsense! That's what they mean.
He's too good for them. Too special. Not like the usual
grubby little beasts they get. They hate the rare, that's
what.

GOVERNESS. Has he said anything to you? About the
school?

MRS. GROSE. Not a word.

GOVERNESS. I wonder if there's been some mistake. Or is
he sometimes bad?

MRS. GROSE. Miles? Bad? Never. No. We'll just keep him
here. *You* can teach him. You've been to the university.
You know as much as that wicked school.

GOVERNESS (*thoughtfully*). Don't . . . don't say anything to Miles about this.

MRS. GROSE. Not if you don't want me to.

GOVERNESS. I won't speak to him either, just yet. I want to see if he trusts me. If he'll come to me of his own accord.

MRS. GROSE. I'm sure he will.

GOVERNESS. Boys *do* get in trouble, after all . . . quite innocently.

MRS. GROSE. Not Miles; like a grown gentleman he is . . . and has always been since he could talk. I must go see to their suppers.

GOVERNESS. I'll be in presently.

(*Mrs. Grose goes. The governess, perturbed, walks to the French windows which open onto the terrace. She steps outside. She pauses, looks up. Her expression changes to one of surprise as a man moves into view on the balcony of the wing opposite. He looks down at her. A wind starts. The figure moves off and the governess returns to the drawing room and goes into the hall. She finds Mrs. Grose.*)

GOVERNESS. Oh, Mrs. Grose . . . tell me, is there someone in the house I haven't met? A man!

MRS. GROSE. No, miss, we've only old William. And he's at the stables right now. No, there's no other man here, though we need a proper butler, I say.

GOVERNESS. How very odd!

MRS. GROSE. What is that, miss?

GOVERNESS. Well, I thought I saw a man just now, standing on the balcony. I saw him quite clearly for a moment. Then he went away.

MRS. GROSE. But there's no one here but us and the children and the maids . . . probably the shadow of a cloud you saw. The twilight plays tricks. I remember once . . .

GOVERNESS. No, I saw a young man.

MRS. GROSE. A young man? A gentleman?

GOVERNESS. No . . . no, I think not. He was really rather frightening. He glared at me in the strangest way, as though he hated me.

MRS. GROSE. I'll call William. We'll have him go up to the balcony. Perhaps it's a thief.

GOVERNESS. I don't think a thief would appear the way he did . . . so openly. (*Shivers.*) It's cold here.

MRS. GROSE. You shouldn't have gone out without a wrap. Come in by the fire. What did he look like exactly?

(*They go into drawing room.*)

GOVERNESS. I saw him for only a moment, but I think he had red hair.

MRS. GROSE. *Red* hair?

GOVERNESS. Yes.

MRS. GROSE. Sharp features? A large face?

GOVERNESS. I believe so, yes.

MRS. GROSE (*with growing horror*). And he was quite slender, wasn't he?

GOVERNESS. Yes . . . yes, he was. Do you know him? Is it someone I haven't met?

MRS. GROSE. Yes, I know him! I know him, and you'll never meet him, thank heaven!

GOVERNESS. Well, what *is* his name? Who is he?

MRS. GROSE. Peter Quint, miss, he was the valet here. The one I just told you about.

GOVERNESS. But I thought you said . . .

MRS. GROSE. That's right, miss. He's dead. Six months ago he died!

Dissolve to the drawing room next morning. Miles sits at a table, doing lessons. The governess sits beside him, brooding. Narration begins.

GOVERNESS'S VOICE. I am not superstitious but I believe the mind has powers none of us suspects. I had, I decided, experienced a waking dream that corresponded only by chance to the description of a man six months in his grave. As a result, I was alarmed not by the apparition but by my own susceptibility. As the days passed, however, I put it in the back of my mind, not mentioning it to the children, not wanting to alarm them. That, perhaps, was an error.

MILES. What was the last question, my dear?

GOVERNESS. The last . . . oh, let me see. I seem to've lost the page.

MILES. You *are* woolgathering today.

GOVERNESS. Certainly not. The last question was: "Establish the relationship between Queen Anne and Sophia, the Electress of Hanover."

MILES. It must be awfully dull for you, buried in the country like this, giving me lessons.

GOVERNESS. You have no idea how I enjoy it.

MILES. You're very sweet. I've always said so.

GOVERNESS. Now really, Miles! *Always* said so . . . I've only been here two weeks . . . and to whom have you said so?

MILES. To Mrs. Grose, to Flora . . . she *dotes* on you. She's a clever little girl, don't you think?

GOVERNESS. You're both very quick.

MILES. That's right. You must'nt flatter us. It will turn our heads and we won't be fit for "the serious game of life," as Mr. Cornelius would say.

GOVERNESS. Mr. Cornelius?

MILES. My house master, at school.

GOVERNESS. Do you like him? Do you like the school?

MILES. I suppose as schools go it's perfectly all right. I wouldn't know; it's my first one, after all.

GOVERNESS. But are you happy there?

MILES. Happy?

GOVERNESS. Yes, do you like it?

MILES. I suppose I do, in a way.

GOVERNESS. Do . . . do you look forward to going back this winter?

MILES. What are you trying to say?

GOVERNESS. I simply want to know, that's all.

MILES. Why? Have you heard things?

GOVERNESS. Should I have?

MILES. I really can't say. But I *do* like the school, though it's not Bly, no other place in the world is like Bly. . . .

GOVERNESS. Have you been to so many places?

(Miles crosses to window.)

MILES. Perhaps not, but I love this house and the woods and the lake . . .

264

GOVERNESS. Miles, what . . . what sort of life did you and Flora lead, before I came?

MILES. The same as now. Mrs. Grose looks after us the way she's always done . . . and our uncle is largely invisible, as he's always been.

GOVERNESS. Did you like Miss Jessel?

MILES (*after a beat*). She was not half so clever as you.

GOVERNESS. Now you mean to turn my head. She died quite suddenly, didn't she?

MILES. I believe so. She was never strong.

GOVERNESS. She died, just after Peter Quint was killed, didn't she?

MILES. Mrs. Grose chatters a lot, doesn't she?

GOVERNESS. I hadn't noticed. Two tragedies all in one year deserve some comment . . . some explanation.

MILES. Explanation? Are tragedies meant to be explained?

GOVERNESS. Perhaps not. Peter Quint was the valet, wasn't he?

MILES. I seem to be getting another headache. It must be the Electress of Hanover. Every time I think of her I feel quite weary.

GOVERNESS. Mrs. Grose tells me Peter Quint was killed in an accident.

MILES. I think I shall get a breath of air.

GOVERNESS. It must've been a great shock to everyone.

MILES. Why, look! The sun is nearly out. I don't want to miss it. I'll be back for tea. (*He goes quickly through the door.*)

GOVERNESS'S VOICE. I was more than ever puzzled. Miles had become a different person when I spoke of Peter

Quint. He was evasive, uneasy. For the first time it occurred to me that he too might be aware of that ghastly presence I had seen on the balcony. But if he had seen it, too, why did he not tell me? Why the strange refusal to discuss Peter Quint? The next day I learned the answer, the dreadful answer, to my question.

> *Dissolve to the lakeside. Flora is alone, playing. The governess appears.*

GOVERNESS'S VOICE. The next afternoon Flora was playing at the lakeside while I gathered reeds to make baskets. As I started to rejoin her by the lake, I realized suddenly that Flora was staring furtively at something across the water. I looked, too . . .

> *Cut to the misty figure of a woman in black, beckoning.*

GOVERNESS'S VOICE. . . . and saw a woman in black, who beckoned to Flora as though she knew her. I was about to ask Flora who the woman was . . .

> *Cut to Flora.*

GOVERNESS'S VOICE. . . . when I saw her look at me so slyly, so challengingly, that I could not speak. *(The governess takes Flora's arm. They start off.)* Instead, we went back to the house in absolute silence, no sound on that chill day but the beating of my own heart in my ears . . . for I knew already that the woman we had seen was Miss Jessel.

*Dissolve to the drawing room that after-
noon. Mrs. Grose and the governess are in
mid-scene.*

MRS. GROSE. Miss, I don't know what to think! I can't believe such a thing.

GOVERNESS. And she knows, that's the worst of it! Flora
knew Miss Jessel was there . . . yet she wouldn't
speak . . . it was as if they had a secret, something
I wasn't to know. Oh, Mrs. Grose! That woman's
face . . . her face!

MRS. GROSE. But, miss, what can we do? What *is* there to
do?

GOVERNESS. I don't know yet. But I do know the children are aware of them, every minute of the day and
night.

MRS. GROSE. Then we must write the Master. We must tell
him everything.

GOVERNESS. But *what* are we to write him? Besides, he's
not in London. A letter wouldn't reach him for a month.
He's far away now, in Africa. No, Mrs. Grose, we must
fight them ourselves, together, here in this house.

MRS. GROSE. Miss, I'm frightened.

GOVERNESS. They want something. *She* wanted something
this afternoon, I could tell. I could feel it . . . the air
was filled with . . . with hunger, like a storm!

MRS. GROSE. But what . . . *what* can they want?

(Miles enters, unobserved. He listens.)

GOVERNESS. The children, Mrs. Grose! That's what they
want, that's what they've come back for!

MILES. And what are you two up to? You look rather piqued, my dear. Are you catching cold?
(The two women start with fright. Miles goes to the fireplace, smilingly, and throws a reed onto the flames.)

> *Dissolve to the governess's bedroom late that night. There are two beds, the smaller one with draperies drawn. In the larger one we see the governess lying in a ray of moonlight.*

GOVERNESS'S VOICE. That night the moon was in its last quarter. The house was very still. There were none of those mysterious sounds one associates with old houses. I remember, before I fell asleep, feeling grateful for Flora's presence in the room. Her little bed was close to mine as though for protection. I awakened shortly after midnight, disturbed by the moonlight in my face. I got up, aware, obscurely, that something was happening in the house. . . .

> *Cut to the long hallway outside the bedroom. Flora is in her nightdress. She signals at the window. Then, hearing the governess, she hides behind a curtain. When the governess has walked past her hiding place, Flora slips back into the bedroom. The governess pauses midway down the hall and looks out the window.*

GOVERNESS'S VOICE. I saw Miles on the terrace, quite alone; he was looking up at the balcony.

Cut to Miles outside on the terrace. He is wearing only a nightshirt. His back is to the governess. But then he turns slowly and looks straight up at her, challengingly.

Dissolve to the drawing room as the governess enters quickly. Miles is already there, waiting.

MILES. I thought you'd be up tonight.

GOVERNESS. What on earth were you doing out there? It's a freezing night! And . . . and where are your slippers?

MILES. I *have* been bad, haven't I?

GOVERNESS. Miles, sit down . . . over here. *(She lights candle.)*

MILES. It's awfully late. You mustn't scold me until morning.

GOVERNESS. I don't intend to scold you. I only want to know if there's anything you'd like to tell me?

MILES. About tonight?

GOVERNESS. About tonight, yes . . . and about all the . . .

MILES *(quickly)*. I wanted to show you that I could be bad, that's all. Just to be different. And the moonlight *is* lovely, isn't it?

GOVERNESS. I meant something else, Miles.

MILES. Oh. . . . My dear, when am I to go back to school? My holidays *are* over. Or did you know?

GOVERNESS. Yes, I knew, but I'm afraid you're not going back to that school.

MILES. And why not?

GOVERNESS. They have refused to take you. They wrote to say that you were a bad influence on the others.

MILES. Oh.

GOVERNESS. I haven't mentioned this until now because I wanted you to tell me yourself what the trouble was.

MILES. There's nothing to tell. Besides, I hated that school. I should prefer a new field, anyway. I'm quite glad they don't want me.

GOVERNESS. Miles, what did you do? You . . . you didn't steal, did you?

MILES. What a silly creature you are, my dear. Of course I didn't . . . not really. It was . . . other things . . . more what I said, stories I told. The boys repeated them. That's all.

GOVERNESS. What sort of stories? Miles, you *must* tell me. I *can* help you. Believe me, I can!

(The door flies open in a gust of wind. The candle goes out. The governess runs to the window as the wind stops. Miles crosses to the table.)

GOVERNESS *(turning to him, pleading)*. Miles, tell me! Please . . . please!

MILES. Tell you what? That it was *I* who blew the candle out?

Dissolve to the downstairs hall the next day. We hear piano music as Mrs. Grose bustles about. The governess's narration begins.

GOVERNESS'S VOICE. The next morning, neither of us mentioned what had happened, and the children, as though by design, were more than ever angelic.

270

Dissolve to the drawing room. The governess is napping while Miles plays the piano.

GOVERNESS'S VOICE. After luncheon, Miles offered to play for me. Tired from lack of sleep, from anxiety, I dozed off. I was not aware when he left the room.

(Miles goes. A moment later, Mrs. Grose enters.)

MRS. GROSE. Oh . . . miss?

GOVERNESS *(sits up with a start)*. I must've been napping. Where's Miles?

MRS. GROSE. I don't know. I thought he was with you. But it's Miss Flora I'm worried about. She's not in her room.

GOVERNESS. But I took her up myself, after lunch, for her nap.

MRS. GROSE. She's gone. I was just there. I've looked in the pantry — she often plays there — but Cook said . . .

GOVERNESS. The lake! Mrs. Grose, she's at the lake! Come . . . quickly!

Dissolve to the lakeside. Flora is playing at the lake's edge. A rowboat has been pulled up to the shore. Mrs. Grose and the governess approach.

FLORA *(demurely)*. You both *are* naughty to be out in the cold like this. I've got my coat. And look at you! Really!

GOVERNESS. You're the naughty one, Flora. You're supposed to be in your room taking your nap, like a good child.

MRS. GROSE. Instead of frightening us half to death. I wonder how that boat got there?

FLORA. I can't think. I should love to go rowing, wouldn't you?

GOVERNESS. Whose boat is it?

MRS. GROSE. Well, it's ours, but no one's used it since Peter . . . since early last summer. It's kept in the boathouse, on the other side. No one ever goes near it.

GOVERNESS. Then I wonder who could've . . . Look! Mrs. Grose . . . look! She's there!

> *Cut to Miss Jessel, standing among the willows.*
> *Cut to Mrs. Grose, bewildered.*

MRS. GROSE. I don't see a thing, miss; there's nothing there . . . but the trees.

GOVERNESS. Woman, she's there, I tell you. Look! Are you blind? Can't you see? Like a blazing fire! *(Turns savagely on Flora.) You* can see her, Flora, *you* can see Miss Jessel, can't you?
(Flora starts to cry.)

MRS. GROSE. There, there, child . . . don't cry. It's all right.

GOVERNESS. She sees her, too, plain as day!

FLORA. Take me back, Mrs. Grose . . . please. . . . Take me away from her.

GOVERNESS. From me?

FLORA. From you!

GOVERNESS. Flora . . .

MRS. GROSE. Stop it, miss! Please! You're frightening the child out of her wits.

FLORA *(screaming)*. Go away! I hate you! I hate you! I hate . . .

GOVERNESS. Take her back to the house, please. Put her to bed. I'll talk to you later.

(Mrs. Grose carries the child off. The governess turns to confront the ghost, but Miss Jessel is gone.)

> *Dissolve to the drawing room that night. Miles sits before the fire, drinking tea, as the governess enters.*

MILES. Have you thought of a new school for me?

GOVERNESS. I have made inquiries, yes. *(She sits opposite him.)*

MILES. I believe I should like a school closer to home.

GOVERNESS. That may not be easy to arrange.

MILES. My uncle will be sad, I suppose, the way I failed him at his old school.

GOVERNESS. I think he has every right to be disappointed, don't you?

MILES. Of course, but then he needn't be disappointed if he never knows.

GOVERNESS. Do you propose I *not* tell him?

MILES. Ah, my dear, you are incorruptible . . . of course you must tell him. Not that we'll ever hear much from him about it . . . I don't think he's too interested in Flora and me.

GOVERNESS. How can you say that? He is most concerned about you.

MILES. I'm sure he'll be concerned once he reads your letter.

GOVERNESS. And how do you know about my letter?

MILES. I assume you wrote him. It's your duty, isn't it

(crosses to window), to tell him the school doesn't want me? No moon tonight. No stars either, all misty. I think I shall take a stroll before supper.

GOVERNESS. *Must* you go out?

MILES. "Must" is not the word, my dear. I *prefer* to go out. I like the night . . . you know that, I think.

(He goes out. Old William, the manservant, enters.)

GOVERNESS. Oh, William, did you do as I asked?

WILLIAM. Yes, miss. Two tickets on the train for London tonight.

GOVERNESS. We'll have an early supper. Have the carriage at the door by seven o'clock.

WILLIAM. Yes, miss. *(He hovers, uncomfortably.)*

GOVERNESS. You have something to say, William?

WILLIAM. Yes, miss, I do. The letter. The one you gave me to post yesterday, the one to the Master, in London.

GOVERNESS. What about it?

WILLIAM. Always I put the letters for the post on the pantry table. It was there in the morning, miss, with the others . . .

GOVERNESS. Do you mean to say you lost it?

WILLIAM. I didn't lose it, but it was gone when the postman came.

GOVERNESS. Then I must write another, that's all. The wind must've blown it away. You'll probably find it one of these days . . .

WILLIAM. There's no wind in the pantry, miss.

GOVERNESS. Thank you, William. Be sure the carriage is on time.

WILLIAM. Yes, miss.

(He leaves the room, passing Mrs. Grose at the door.)

GOVERNESS. Is Flora better?

MRS. GROSE. Worse . . . worse . . . oh, miss, she's terrible!

GOVERNESS. She has no fever, I hope.

MRS. GROSE. No, no fever. If only she had. You were right. You *are* right. I'm blind, that's all . . . a simple fool.

GOVERNESS. Come, you are no such thing.

MRS. GROSE. You should hear her. You should hear what she says. She's not a child . . . she's like a madwoman . . . and the things she says, you wouldn't believe!

GOVERNESS. What sort of things?

MRS. GROSE. I couldn't repeat them, not ever! Such horror . . . and a child, too, a baby saying them, *raving* like the devil was in her. Oh, miss, where . . . *where* could she've known such things?

GOVERNESS. Old William is bringing the carriage around after supper. You'll take the night train to London, you and Flora. You'll go straight to Harley Street, to the house.

MRS. GROSE. To London? But how . . . I mean, the Master . . .

GOVERNESS. It's *my* responsibility. I'll explain to him. Flora must not stay here another night. Do you understand?

MRS. GROSE. Yes, miss, I understand. I'll get our things ready. *(A beat.)* What . . . what about Miles?

GOVERNESS. He'll stay here with me.

Dissolve to the drawing room that night. We hear narration as the governess and Miles face one another before the fire.

GOVERNESS'S VOICE. I was determined to discover the truth, to save Miles if I could from that evil creature whose unnatural presence fell across our lives like the shadow of great wings. I would fight him. I would exorcise him. *I would save Miles!*

MILES. So now we're alone, my dear. You and I.

GOVERNESS. Yes, it would seem that we are.

MILES. Was it really so necessary for them to leave Bly?

GOVERNESS. It was quite necessary; Flora is ill. She will have proper doctors in London.

MILES. Perhaps I should've gone too . . . though I rather like the old place, even in winter.

GOVERNESS. Do you need a doctor, Miles? Is *that* what you need?

MILES. Well, now that you mention it, I don't feel awfully hearty, no.

GOVERNESS. If you like, we can go to London tomorrow. But first we have things to discuss.

MILES. Oh, *ever* so many things! We shall never run out of things to talk about, shall we?

GOVERNESS. I'm not a fool, Miles. You already know that *I* know.

MILES. You mean about the school?

GOVERNESS. Not about the school . . . and not about the letter of mine you stole.

MILES. I *did* make a slip that time, didn't I?

GOVERNESS. It is dishonest to steal letters.

MILES. I am sorry, but I . . . I was curious. I wanted to see what you thought of me.

GOVERNESS. Were you impressed by what I said?

276

MILES. I thought you . . . more than kind, my dear.

GOVERNESS. Thank you. There will, of course, be other letters to your uncle.

MILES. More's the pity. I tore up a good one.

GOVERNESS. But I'm not concerned with the letters *or* with
the school right now. I want to know something else.

MILES. Something else?

GOVERNESS. I want you to tell me about this house.

(Miles gets to his feet, uneasily.)

MILES. I'm awfully tired tonight. I think I shall go up to
bed now.

GOVERNESS. Not until we've talked. Not until you've told
me.

MILES. I . . . I'll tell you tomorrow, on the train. That'll
make the trip go faster. . . .

GOVERNESS *(crossing to him)*. It *must* be tonight. Miles,
Miles, this is the only way . . . you must be honest . . .
you *must* let me help you fight them . . . and we
can . . . we really can!

MILES. I *do* feel awfully odd. I think I'd better go up to
bed. Good night, my dear.

GOVERNESS. Then you give up, just like that? Oh, Miles, tell
me!

MILES *(fiercely)*. I can't. Don't you see? I can't! You must
leave it be! I mean, there's nothing to tell, nothing to
know . . . till tomorrow.

*(The French windows burst open with a crash. The cur-
tains billow in a sudden wind. Miles turns; the governess holds him protectively as she addresses the night.)*

GOVERNESS *(triumphantly)*. You're too late!

MILES. Is it *she?*

GOVERNESS. No, it's not she . . . it's the other, but he can't take you now. I shan't let him. Never again!
(Miles tears away from her and goes onto the terrace. She follows him.)

> *Cut to the terrace. The wind is blowing.*
> *Miles looks above him, blindly.*

MILES. I can't see! Where is he? Tell me, you devil, where is he? *Where is Peter Quint?*

GOVERNESS. He's out there, in the night, waiting! But he can't have you, not now! You're not his any more. You're mine, my darling, mine! But look at him, look at him, see what he is. For the last time, *look!*
(Miles crosses unsteadily to the balcony; then, abruptly, he stops, he turns, he raises his hands as though drowning and falls face forward to the ground. She runs to him. She gathers him in her arms. The wind stops.)

GOVERNESS'S VOICE. And so it was, in that great moment of final freedom, he died. His little heart, dispossessed, had stopped.

> *Fade out on the governess, the dead child*
> *in her arms.*